What Your Relationship with Your Dog Reveals about You

Dogology

VICKI CROKE AND SARAH WILSON

RODALE

Rodale books may be purchased for business or promotional use or for special sales. For information, please write to:

Special Markets Department, Rodale Inc., 733 Third Avenue, New York, NY 10017

Printed in the United States of America

Rodale Inc. makes every effort to use acid-free ⊗, recycled paper ♻.

Interior photo credits appear on page 233

Book design by Joanna Williams

Library of Congress Cataloging-in-Publication Data

Croke, Vicki.
    Dogology : what your relationship with your dog reveals about you / Vicki Croke and Sarah Wilson.
        p.   cm.
    Includes index.
    ISBN-13 978–1–59486–920–4 hardcover
    ISBN-10 1–59486–920–0 hardcover
    1. Dog owners—Psychology.   2. Dogs—Psychological aspects.   3. Human-animal relationships.   I. Wilson, Sarah, date   II. Title.
SF422.7.C76   2008
636.7—dc22   2008036643

Distributed to the trade by Macmillan

2   4   6   8   10   9   7   5   3   1   hardcover

We inspire and enable people to improve their lives and the world around them

For more of our products visit **rodalestore.com** or call 800-848-4735

For all the dogs in our lives
who've shown us not only who we are
but who we can be.

Contents

Part 1: What's Your Type?

Part 2: What's Your Breed?

What's Your Type?

Introduction

Throughout the past several thousand years, we have tried to understand and organize personality types using the stars, skull shapes, tea leaves, and the human mind. Astrology, phrenology, tassology, psychology. Finally, there is a more reliable—if often higher-shedding—system for understanding yourself and the other two-legged creatures around you: Dogology. Yes, dogs. Who better to reveal our souls than the creatures who have seen us exercise naked on the mini-trampoline, watched us eat Cherry Garcia at home alone after a dinner date, or heard us sing the Chipmunks' version of "Funkytown" at the tops of our lungs?

Yes, your worst nightmare—and fondest dream—have come true. Dogs can talk.

And we—Vicki Croke and Sarah Wilson, the world's first practicing Dogologists—have been jotting it all down, forming this foolproof personality-analyzing system.

Do you realize just how exposed your deepest emotions are when expressed in your unguarded interactions with your dog? Well, you will.

And you might be a little more cautious about some of the things you say to your dog in front of other people. If we pay attention, our relationships with our dogs—how we choose them, what traits we are attracted to, what we see in them, what we expect from them, what we give them, what we withhold, how we punish and how we praise, the way we interpret their desires—will tell us a great deal about our own psyches.

Who needs constant reassurance? ("Come here, baby, Mommy needs a hug.") Who gets a kick from control? ("Off that couch, pronto. Why? Because I said so!") Which owner has childhood scars that leave her feeling perennially at risk? ("You won't let anyone near me, will you, Peaches?")

We relate to other humans—spouses, kids, parents, bosses—in a fairly uniform manner. We are strong or weak, talkative or quiet. We are loving or withdrawn, quick-tempered or patient. Confident or unsure of ourselves. You could psychoanalyze yourself through interpreting the complex ways you deal with other people. In fact, in part, that's exactly what shrinks do. But there's an easier way. A shortcut. A very sweet cheat sheet. You want to know what kind of daughter, parent, or spouse you are? Check out how patient, kind, doting, or aloof you are with your dog.

Through our dogs we can get a remarkably clear signal—it's the difference between high-def and analog. That's because our interactions with our dogs tend to be so unconscious, so bare, and so basic. Because our relationships with our dogs are so much simpler than with fellow humans and less muddied by commentary and feedback about our own behavior and choices, we are much less self-conscious when we interact with our dogs. Dogs are close to the ultimate "I'm OK, You're OK" relational mirror, and we can learn a lot about ourselves from the way we connect to them. We just have to tune in a little to something we normally don't think much about.

But do ponder it for a second. Vicki finds that in an office setting, she's not always great at sizing up the personality of a new co-worker. But put her in a dog park and surround her with people and their dogs? Then she can psychoanalyze at 50 paces! The guy who orders his Rhodesian to heel every time the dog gets more than three feet away? A person who uses control to manage his worries (we bet his sock drawer is a thing of beauty). The woman in the L.L. Bean rain gear chucking the ball for her Aussie for hours at a time? A very responsible perfectionist. The hippie lawyer who shrugs and smiles indulgently as her Labrador wallows in yet another mud hole? Vicki's kind of friend! Sarah finds that she can often nail aspects of someone's past by the issues they have in training. Get stressed out and tense learning a new physical skill? Did you have some gym teacher make a sport out of criticism? Or an older sibling who mocked your early efforts? How about someone who praises very little? He may simply be repeating the low-praise practice of his family without any awareness that he is doing so. The deepest patterns we have are often the hardest for us to see—they are our emotional "air": always present, never thought about. Everyone is shaped by his or her history; learn what to look for and you will see the echoes left behind wherever you look.

What we've done in *Dogology* is to organize and clarify all those gut feelings most of us have when observing the interaction of different personality types with their dogs. And we're certain you'll recognize them.

For one thing, once we sorted them out, guess what? They had many of the hallmarks of other systems such as astrological signs or personality-testing types. Where other systems have "Virgo" or "Questioner" or "INFJ," we've got "the Expert." Of course, the dog slant has given us a whole different kind of interplay to work with and think about.

Dogology is meant to be a key that will open a door to an amazing world of enlightenment. With this system, you'll be able to recognize and learn a little bit about yourself and all the other dog owners around you. It will help you to understand yourself a little better, to be a better pet parent, and to better connect with all other creatures—humans included.

We've broken our personality profiles into three zones: Feelers, Thinkers, and Do-ers. Then within each zone are three types, for a total of nine types.

Feelers

ANGEL: nurturing, focused on her dogs' needs

SOUL MATE: warm, deep-feeling, and into the connection with her dog

FREE SPIRIT: open-minded and looking for a boundary-free and stress-free relationship with her dog

Thinkers

IDEALIST: sets high standards for herself and her dog

EXPERT: earnest and into knowing all she can about her dog

OBSERVER: analytical and fascinated by her dog's behavior

Do-ers

DYNAMO: energetic and reliable about the dog's schedule

MASTER: disciplined and eager to forge a bond with her dog through work they both love

BUDDY: wired for fun and into sharing adventure with her dog

In the portraits of each, we provide quickie lists for instant identification—how to tell where you fit. We identify and celebrate your strengths, and we also provide gentle challenge exercises to overcome your . . . uh . . . gaps in perfection.

We know that you will see all your friends in these type profiles. And we hope that when you're not laughing in recognition, you'll be gasping at the insights—into your own behavior and that of those around you. ("There's Mary! The Standard Poodle! The spotless anorak! The collapsible water dish that matches Portia's collar!" Or more important: "So that's why I accuse my husband of ignoring Bailey!")

We're also sure that just as with other systems, you'll find that you really identify with one type, but that there are elements in your personality that resonate with one or two other types. So you may find yourself majoring in Expert and minoring in Soul Mate. Maybe an Angel with a hot Free Spirit streak. Or an Idealist with a touch of Dynamo.

If you want to focus on finding what type you are yourself, begin at "Welcome to Your Dogology Neighborhood" on page 9. Through a series of fun quizzes, you can situate yourself within the right zone and then sniff out your exact type.

Our canine cosmology wouldn't be complete without a very thorough tour of dog breeds and what our attraction to specific kinds means. You're a plus-size model with an Italian Greyhound? A librarian with an Airedale? A sales rep who likes Dalmatians or an actress with a Doodle? We'll tell you what it all means—and even what to think about a date who owns a Chinese Crested.

We've got lots of other little insight paths for you to wander down. How about a field guide to all the regulars you see at the dog park? Want to know how much the words you use to praise your dog can tell you about your own vulnerabilities? How the breeds of dog you're drawn toward can show you the kind of mate you'd be happiest with? Why examining your relationship with your dog can help you become a happier, more content, and confident person? Then start reading anywhere.

Dogology is a fun road map to your heart, your dog, your pals, and virtually everyone you meet when you (and they) are holding one end of a leash.

Typecasting

Why wait until all your friends have read the book and already have you typecast? (Hmmm, that could be trouble.) Beat them all to the punch by diving in here and using our foolproof Dogology GPS.

The fastest way to get you to your Dogology "home" type is first to find the larger Dogology neighborhood you live in. There are three distinct zones—emotional, intellectual, and action-oriented. Our quiz will guide you in.

Welcome to Your Dogology Neighborhood

1) I'd rather spend a day at home:
   a. Napping with a good book
   b. Talking to friends
   c. Doing outside chores

2) My favorite TV shows are generally:
   a. Soap operas/sitcoms
   b. Sports/adventure/reality
   c. PBS/how-to/the arts

3) When I go shopping, I:

    a. Read the labels/compare prices

    b. Buy what I'm hungry for

    c. Wish I were doing something else

4) My best friends are:

    a. Ones I've had for years

    b. Friends I do things with

    c. Friends with whom I can really debate things and talk things through

5) My favorite way to spend time with my dog is:
   a. Teaching her something new
   b. Reading some new dog magazines, with him at my feet
   c. Cuddling with her

6) If my boss is hassling me, I want to:
   a. Scream at him. But instead I go home, call my friend, and cry
   b. Lecture him. But instead I go home and call my friends to talk and talk and talk about it
   c. Walk out. But instead I take a "mental health day" and call it a "sick day"

7) If a friend comes to me with a problem, I am most likely to:
   a. Talk it over, discovering the root cause of his upset
   b. Talk it over logically, giving suggestions and options
   c. Invite him to go do something else with me to get his mind off it

Answers:
1) a. Thinker, b. Feeler, c. Do-er
2) a. Feeler, b. Do-er, c. Thinker
3) a. Thinker, b. Feeler, c. Do-er
4) a. Feeler, b. Do-er, c. Thinker
5) a. Do-er, b. Thinker, c. Feeler
6) a. Feeler, b. Thinker, c. Do-er
7) a. Feeler, b. Thinker, c. Do-er

If you answered four or more times in one zone, go to it now. (Pay attention to any other zones that showed up more than once—these will help you see other aspects of your personality. Many of us have a leash in at least two zones.)

If your answers are pretty evenly distributed among the three zones, read each one and find the one you're most comfortable in. Some people straddle a few territories; there's nothing wrong with that—in fact, there might be quite a bit right with being so well-rounded!

Once in your zone, you'll be asked five questions. If you answer three or more as one type, you're there! If you have two or fewer answers as a type, read each of the types to see which you're drawn toward.

Emotional: The Feeler

Dogology Types: Angel, Soul Mate, Free Spirit

This trinity leads from the heart.

Usual Strengths

- Intuitive

- Empathic

- Recognizes and rejoices in connection

- Accepts idiosyncrasies as charming foibles in loved ones

Possible Weaknesses

- Easily distracted—what some would call "flaky"

- Can find it hard to set reasonable limits on behavior

- Guilty of "relentless understanding"

- Spend more time dreaming (or worrying) than doing

Angel, Soul Mate, or Free Spirit?

Take the following quiz:

1) My friend has a spat with her significant other. I'm most likely to:
   a. Remind her of the good times they've had and what they have in common.
   b. Go over her dating history and underline the losers she's been with.
   c. Talk things through with her, but lighten things up with a little laughter.

2) I'm late for a doctor's appointment:
   a. Couldn't be me, I don't often go to the doctor. I am, however, at the veterinarian's office for one reason or another virtually every month.
   b. I think about calling, but why? I've been going to them for years, they know me well, and I'm always late, so the office staff just expects me to arrive late.
   c. I call up and sincerely apologize, telling them I'll be there in five minutes—of course, I'm actually ten minutes away and I know that—what I don't know is why I said five.

3) During the holidays, I want to be:
   a. At home with my family.
   b. Spending time with my friends—I consider them my "real" family.
   c. Drinking heavily.

4) When I remember my childhood, my first thought is:
   a. My family puts the "d" in dysfunction.
   b. Basically I had a good one.
   c. I try not to dwell on my childhood.

5) At night, my dog is:

   a. Under the covers or on the pillow, of course.

   b. Sleeping wherever she can find a spot on the bed; it's crowded up there.

   c. Anywhere she wants—I don't think I understand this question.

Answers:

1) a. Soul Mate, b. Angel, c. Free Spirit

2) a. Angel, b. Free Spirit, c. Soul Mate

3) a. Soul Mate, b. Free Spirit, c. Angel

4) a. Free Spirit, b. Soul Mate, c. Angel

5) a. Soul Mate, b. Angel, c. Free Spirit

Intellectual: The Thinker

Dogology Types: Idealist, Expert, Observer

The trio that relies on brainpower.

Usual Strengths	Possible Weaknesses
🐾 Logical	🐾 May not recognize or appreciate emotional perspectives
🐾 Thinks things out (sometimes after reacting emotionally)	🐾 Prone to distraction—easily lost in thought
🐾 Can develop and then implement that plan	🐾 Can be immobilized when seeking the "best" answer
🐾 Tends to see to the heart of the matter—cutting through confusion	🐾 Prone to being judgmental
🐾 Pragmatic	🐾 Pragmatic (Hey, wasn't this a strength above? Yes, well, you know the yin and yang thing. While this kind of logical reasoning can be incredibly helpful, in some situations it is perceived by others as cold.)

Idealist, Expert, or Observer?

Take the following quiz:

1) My friend has a spat with her significant other. I'm most likely to:
   a. Remind her of the life she has built with this person.
   b. Speak to her about the common ups and downs of relationships.
   c. Listen attentively.

2) I'm late for a doctor's appointment:
   a. My heart sinks, but I make a note of where the problem was and how to avoid it in the future.
   b. I call in, feeling the burn of shame, to give the estimated time of arrival and explain that there was a traffic tie-up (and there was).
   c. I notice that I'm late as I pull into the parking lot—I got a bit lost in thought. That happens . . .

3) At night, my dog is:
   a. At the foot of my bed, on her dog blanket—it's best if dogs can bond with you at night.
   b. Sleeping on her bed. I read that it's best if dogs sleep lower than you.
   c. Sleeping in her crate, of course—it's best if dogs sleep in their "dens."

4) I have an impossibly long list of things to do today. I look at the list and:
   a. Prioritize it, deciding what needs to be done first and what can wait.
   b. Figure I'll do what I can today, then do the rest tomorrow. Nothing is that important.
   c. Shorten it to a doable length and then get at it—completely logical.

5) If I have a knotty problem, I'd rather:

    a. Talk it over with close friends or family.

    b. Mull on it for a while.

    c. Hop on the Internet and research it.

Answers:

1) a. Idealist, b. Expert, c. Observer

2) a. Expert, b. Idealist, c. Observer

3) a. Idealist, b. Expert, c. Observer

4) a. Observer, b. Expert, c. Idealist

5) a. Idealist, b. Observer, c. Expert

Action-Oriented: The Do-er

Dogology Types: Dynamo, Master, Buddy

These three types throw their whole bodies into the effort.

Usual Strengths

- Takes action

- Is a natural leader

- Great in a crisis

- Rarely boring

- Mentally quick

Possible Weaknesses

- May take action before understanding either the problem or the solution

- May not recognize or take the time for emotional connection

- Sees others as "overly sensitive"—translation: Their reactions make no sense to the do-er

- Can be seen by others as distant or lacking in empathy

Dynamo, Master, or Buddy?

Take the following quiz:

1) My friend has a spat with her significant other. I'm most likely to:
   a. Grab her hand and head to the mall for a little shopping therapy.
   b. Help him understand his part in this and what he can do to change the dynamic.
   c. Take my friend out for an adventure—get moving.

2) I'm late for a doctor's appointment:
   a. It's only a few minutes; what's the big deal?
   b. I call ahead, explaining that I'm running errands and got delayed.
   c. I stress out because I'm as good as my word and I hate being late.

3) At night, my dog:
   a. Sleeps curled against me. I love that.
   b. Totally hogs the bed. I can't imagine how one dog can take up so much room!
   c. Is off the bed and sleeps on whichever dog bed he wants.

4) The cutest thing my dog does is:
   a. When I tell her "down," she leaps in the air and then drops like a stone.
   b. When running through the woods, he stops and looks back at me—waiting for me to catch up.
   c. Rests her head on my lap and gazes up at me when I am driving.

5) I have an impossibly long list of things to do today. I look at the list and:
   a. Rearrange it so I can do it efficiently.

b. I speed up, because when the going gets tough, the tough get going.

c. I shrug. I'll do what I can, but I won't give up that time with a friend—everything can wait; it's not the end of the world.

Answers:

1) a. Dynamo, b. Master, c. Buddy
2) a. Buddy, b. Dynamo, c. Master
3) a. Dynamo, b. Buddy, c. Master
4) a. Master, b. Buddy, c. Dynamo
5) a. Dynamo, b. Master, c. Buddy

The Dogology Types

By now, having taken the Dogology GPS quizzes, you have likely zeroed in on your type. Read on to discover the defining characteristics of each type. If you're still torn between two or more types, scan all the types that are calling to you. Remember: Your whole personality does not have to fit into just one type. Most of us have a primary type and carry another one or two subtypes in smaller roles. You may major in Observer and minor in Master, for instance.

Even once you know your type, and likely the types of all your dog-walking pals, we hope you'll return to this section again and again as you and your dog continue to explore the world and meet new people. You may find that later as you reread the section, different parts of the profiles will resonate with you.

The Soul Mate

Motto: Love me, love my dog!

Soul Mates, true to their Feeler selves, just love to love. They revel in being with their dogs. This is a grand life for a dog—thoughtfully tended, trained, and always included—the type of life that made a homeless man look at a friend with her dog and heartbreakingly inquire: "Can I be your dog?" (Hell, if you're a Soul Mate, you've heard boyfriends and grandmothers say the same!)

Whenever a Soul Mate says "we," the translation is "me and the dog"—*we* are going for a walk, then down to Three Dog Bakery, and after that, maybe *we'll* come home, read the paper, and nap. Note to two-legged significant others: For a long time after you appear on the horizon, "we" will still mean the dog and the Soul Mate, and things you guys do together will be announced as "Bob and I are planning to have lunch after 'we' go to the park." Case in point, this write-up:

My relationship with my dog is one of the things I treasure most in my life. I compete in obedience, and the most important factor contributing to our success is the relationship we have. I cannot say that I have not made mistakes, but I have come to realize how important an honest relationship is. If there ever came a time when we no longer enjoyed obedience, I

Soul Mate's advice: Let sleeping dogs lie, ideally on my lap! ➤

can truly say that we would be just as happy staying at home, lying on the bed, and watching movies.

Quintessentially Soul Mate—we hear how much she values the connection to her dog, how their success is a shared one, and that mutual enjoyment is critical to her own enjoyment of the activity. The human takes responsibility for her mistakes and doesn't blame the dog for them in the least. She goes on to make it clear that when the dog no longer has fun, then they will have fun doing other things together. While they enjoy competition, it doesn't define their connection. It's a loving write-up from a classic Soul Mate.

Many of us seem to have at least a little Soul Mate in our characters, especially if we treat our dogs like children. Now, this is completely understandable when we consider that caring for a child can be the template for caring for a pet—whether or not you have children of your own. For many women, regardless of their own actual mothering experience, cradling a puppy or small dog in their arms and looking down into an adorable face can cause maternal urges to arise rapidly and sometimes unexpectedly. So, the Soul Mate either makes the dog her friend or her child (with friendship woven in).

At their best, Soul Mates have a deep connection based on respect for the dog's unique self. Empathetic and attentive, Soul Mates tend to know what their dogs need almost before the dogs do. They are very well taken care of and their safety is always a top priority.

The Soul Mate's dog also gets to go places and do things. Soul Mates find vacation spots that allow pets. They eat at outdoor cafés where dogs are sanctioned. And because he has been doing it since he was a pup, he is well socialized and comfortable at work, in the car, and even at dinner parties. If you want to keep a Soul Mate as a friend, her dog will always be welcome at any social event you host. And make sure the request is sincere and robust (nothing tepid will do): "You MUST bring Elliott!"

A strong bond between these two is a lovely thing to behold. With the Soul Mate, there is no middle ground:

I love my Sheltie beyond all reason. He is my child. He taught me how to love totally and unconditionally while expecting nothing in return. He loves me as much as I love him; it's as though we are soul mates. He gets the best of everything, and his health, happiness, and well-being are my top priority. He is loving, sweet, gentle, kind, tenderhearted, smart, and beautiful. I adore him! Our long walks every day help to keep us both fit and healthy. He is my very best friend, and I am his very best friend.

Some might see this as a romanticized view of the "other." But the right combination of dog (one who can handle that amount of adulation) and Soul Mate can lead to a pretty perfect union.

A Soul Mate can experience a kind of bliss with her dog that meditating monks would find enviable. Happiness for a Soul Mate is a long drive on a sunny day with great music playing and not a care in the world; she looks over at her companion dog—sleepy-eyed, content, perfect in every hair and whisker—and she is content. Walks on the beach, time in front of the fire with a book, even trips to the grocery store are heavenly because her trusted shadow is steadfastly by her side.

This is a team that is totally attuned to one another. In harmony and in love. Whole days can pass by in a kind of soft-focus sweet dream for these two. Their lives are very much entwined.

While the death of a dog is devastating to every owner, a Soul Mate can often reach extreme levels of despair and may not be able to contemplate another dog for a long, long time. This bond often has felt like a marriage, a very good marriage, and dating will be the last thing on the Soul Mate's mind when she loses her dear companion. After a very long grieving period, many Soul Mates will begin to consider loving again, but will also go through a lengthy, complicated phase of feeling guilty for even having such thoughts.

So, when the Soul Mate does get a pup and you meet the new bundle of joy, be sure to EMOTE! Choosing this particular pup was a lightning-bolt moment for her, and that must be acknowledged. But beware: Don't allow your enthusiasm for the new pup to in any way seem to eclipse your feelings for the Soul Mate's last dog. (It's a battle she's waging with herself.)

The slippery slope for Soul Mates is a slide into emotional projection—noted trainer (and Sarah's husband) Brian Kilcommons says this can lead to something that is more of a hostage situation than a relationship.

Projection comes in two common varieties: dog as spokesman for your feelings and dog as representative of your fears.

The first is reminiscent of a series of cartoons from the old *Mad* magazine in which a person's shadow exposes what they are really thinking—you know, the guy politely talking to a beautiful woman while his silhouette leers at hers. Substitute dog for shadow here, and you see that the way you describe your dog's emotions can be very revealing of how you yourself feel. "Bailey really missed you," someone may say to a returning spouse, or "Bailey is mad at you for being late." We all do a little of this, but a true Projectionist is so blinded by her own shtick, she doesn't see who the dog really is.

Soul Mates love to bring their dogs. This young terrier is leashed. Such wisdom is not universal, so put the breakables out of harm's way. ➤

The second kind of Projectionist casts his or her fears onto the dog. They see the dog not as a creature with her own emotions, but as the holder of the owner's painful emotions from the past (you know, those memory-triggered emotions that are as strong decades after the fact). If you grew up in a critical household, you may be concerned that your dog is judging you. While most of us dip a toe into these waters from time to time, the pure Projectionist is doing the backstroke in them.

Real Soul Mates are the poets of the dog-loving world. Their love for their dogs is a sonnet, a song, a psalm, even. They have so much to give, so much joy, attention, acceptance, and appreciation, that all of us would do well to cultivate at least a little of this type in ourselves. And it seems that a healthy portion of dog lovers do carry around at least a slice of Soul Mate.

You May Be a Soul Mate If:

- You see the dog's behavior as a reflection of your own soul.
- You not only allow the dog on all furniture but also encourage him to get up there. And

furniture includes the bed even when you are having sex. You fit the bill if your partner makes the dog get off the bed despite your protests. And you are a charter member of Club Soul Mate if a) that derails the sex for you or b) you stay mad about it during the sex.

- You speak for your dog about him "missing Daddy" or "being mad at Mommy."
- You feel abandoned if the dog lies in another room.
- You idealize your dog's actions. Other people have "fun" or "wild" dogs; you have a "noble" dog.
- Your dog doesn't ever just "drop" the ball; he "gives" it to less fortunate dogs.
- You carry a portfolio of dog pictures covering birth to present, and if the viewer tries to skip ahead, you'll stop him: "Wait! Wait! You missed one!"

You're *Not* a True Soul Mate If You:

- Are embarrassed to hold your dog in the breast-feeding position.
- Avoid talking baby talk to your dog in public.
- Use a crate without regret or personal recrimination.
- Have ever sent out a holiday card sans your dog on it.
- Think doggy birthday parties are silly.
- Banish the dog from the bedroom when you are feeling romantic, then tell him to "Knock it off" if he whines at the door.

You May Be Headed for Trouble If:

- When you flare up at your dog, you actually blame the dog.
- You think your dog is doing things to annoy you or get you upset.

- You believe your dog "knows better" or is "stubborn" or "stupid."
- Despite aggressive or obnoxious behavior, you still refer to your dog as "your baby" or "Mommy's little boy."
- When your dog goes tail-wagging forward to greet another friendly dog, you pull her back (better yet, scoop her up) while exclaiming in a panicked voice to the other owner: "No! She's scared of other dogs!"

Favorite Names

Words that reflect your affection for this little bug: Sugar, Angel, Babydoll. Characters from your favorite children's books: Madeline, Eloise, George, Roo, Piglet. May be named after poets (Longfellow—ideal for Dachshunds!) or musicians who died tragically young (Cobain), or romantic figures from great literature (Romeo—half the fun is calling him: "Romeo! Romeo! Wherefore art thou, Romeo?"). Classic folk songs are naming gold mines too—like Clementine.

Sweet Nothings

When he's praised, the Soul Mate's dog is told he is the baby, sweetie pie, honeybun, cupcake (and any number of other dessert analogies—a cultural habit that really deserves a bit of study should any reader feel the urge).

Tips for Training

Look into Tellington-Touch (T-Touch)—its hands-on approach with specific tasks and special equipment may fascinate you. It *requires* you to touch your dog—a lot. Could there be anything better?

Character-Building Exercises

- Stop calling your adult dog a puppy for one month.
- Speak in a normal tone of voice for one week.
- When you want to pet your dog, call her over; don't rush cooing across the room for ~~one month~~ . . . okay ~~one week~~ . . . okay, okay, shoot for a day.

Breeds to Which Soul Mates Are Drawn

Almost any breed can fit here.

The Soul Mate's choice is deeply personal—it is always a "one in a million" connection. True Soul Mates fall for whomever they fall for—sometimes it's a breed that cuts a dashing figure as a sidekick—a Deerhound (like Karen Blixen's Dusk in *Out of Africa*) or a noble Nordic perhaps. Or maybe they want company curling up for a long afternoon of reading, where a Basset might fill the bill. The projecting type of Soul Mate picks dogs who allow near complete projection. For Pet Parents, there's a bias for roundheaded, big-eyed, baby-faced breeds, such as Shih Tzus, Pugs, or Boston Terriers.

Breeds Soul Mates Should Avoid

Independent dogs who want to do their own thing may not fulfill the Soul Mate's need to connect. Lhasa Apsos, Akitas, and Canaan Dogs all may need more "alone time" than works for this human and may find her attempts to drag them up onto her lap bizarre and unwelcome.

The Soul Mate in Love

SOUL MATE—Possible, but volatile. Need at least two dogs in the household, possibly three, to pull off this dynamic, so no one has to feel rejected or threatened if her dog focuses on the other. If this all can be managed, this can be the lovey-dovey couple that makes others yell, "Get a room!"

EXPERT—The Soul Mate sees the world almost exclusively in emotional terms, while the Expert likes to weigh things rationally when possible. If they appreciate each other (especially if they both have an intellectual streak, and the Expert has a soulful streak), great. If they don't, it could be revolvers at 30 paces at dawn.

DYNAMO—You can try it, but we don't have much hope. Similar to the Idealist, the Dynamo is likely to be dismissed as being a member of the "owner" category. And that's a lifetime sentence, no hope of parole.

ANGEL—Careful now—things could degenerate into competitive compassion. The Soul Mate is really an Angel in a monogamous relationship, so together they can be simpatico or simply loco.

IDEALIST—First of all, no Soul Mate worth the title would ever hang out with an "owner" (she considers herself a "guardian"). But more important, there is a fundamental chasm between these two. The Idealist runs a meritocracy, and the Soul Mate has no expectation beyond "be true to yourself" and "love me totally."

MASTER—Hmmm . . . has potential if the Master allows others to take their own journey and the Soul Mate understands the benefits of education. But if the Master is sliding toward Warden and the Soul Mate is easing toward Projectionist, each will think the other is in need of serious psychiatric intervention (and each may be right).

FREE SPIRIT—If the Soul Mate sees responsibility as one of the primary aspects of caring for the dog, then the "Free" part of Free Spirit is going to cause trouble. Even at their best,

TRUE FRIENDS

One of the things dogs do better than any other companion animal is match our expressions and emotions. That's what our human friends do too (or should). We bounce into a room happy, and they smile, ready to get happy with us. We walk in close-mouthed and serious, and they ask what is wrong. Our dogs do the canine equivalent.

In this picture, we have two happy beings—both with relaxed open mouths with slightly closed eyes. This is a shared expression of joy—a mutual exchange of emotion.

Notice how close they are to each other—relaxed bodies pressed together, heads touching. They are in what's called the intimate zone—the space we reserve for the people we trust the most, those we like the most, those we love. Look at this picture and you know that the pair is happily simpatico: It is obvious, it is beyond question.

the potential for competitive attachment (each vying to be the dog's "best friend") is great. Proceed with caution.

OBSERVER—Possible if the Soul Mate knows the Observer is a bit of an emotional Peeping Tom and she likes to emote with the shades up.

BUDDY—Could be a bucolic bond—if the Soul Mate has an outdoorsy aspect that meets the Buddy's lust for nature. Then, these two could happily camp their way through life.

DOG TALK

"Who woves her widdoo binkie?"

All of us speak to our dogs in a little bit of baby talk. And even if that quote makes you cringe, you have to admit that you are guilty of uttering some version of it around your dog. We all do it, but why?

Well, we know baby talk is an important tool in the development of infants. As studied by social scientists, it is known as motherese, and it follows certain fairly universal patterns as adults use the lilting dialogue to help babies learn about language, conversation, and social interchange.

When we talk to our pets in this form—which some experts refer to as doggerel (as a spoof on the term for clichéd poetry) or pet-ese—we find it does have a lot in common with motherese.

Gail F. Melson explains it in her brilliant book *Why the Wild Things Are: Animals in the Lives of Children* (Harvard University Press): "Much like 'motherese,' the conversational form of speech mothers (and other humans) use toward babies, people speak to their pets in a higher-pitched, soft singsong, often ending an utterance with a rising inflection, as if posing a question, and inserting pauses for imaginary replies. Speech tempo slows, and the length of utterances shortens."

As we do with babies, we tend to fill in the pets' responses for them. As in, "Who's a good girl?" then, "I'm a good girl, Mom!" In one family we know of, which consists of a mother, a teenage son, and two dogs, the boy one day objected to his mother constantly voicing pretend conversations between the dogs. "Mom," he said to her, "am I really that boring that you have to resort to this?"

Well, the mother isn't resorting to anything. The fact is that this is a very important form of communication. One might argue that with babies, there's a point to it all—eventually the baby will talk back. Without that expectation in dogs, are we just being idiots?

It turns out, the answer is no. Melson goes on to cogently explain in *Why the Wild Things Are* that there are some very important differences between motherese and what she calls pet-ese: "When adults have been observed talking to their dogs or birds, they place their heads close to the animal's head and invariably stroke, nuzzle, and pet the animal, seemingly compelled to combine touch and talk. Adults lower their voices to a confidential murmur and their facial muscles relax. With eyes half-closed, a subtle, Mona Lisa–like smile may play across the face. By contrast, adults speaking to babies have more animated, wide-eyed expressions, with tenser facial muscles. . . . Babytalk is less often fused with close physical contact than is talk to pets."

These differences, Melson says, reveal it to be "an affirmation of the bond between animal and human owner."

We're not delusional—we're not futilely attempting to teach dogs to talk, and we're not role-playing mommy with the dog substituting as baby. We are bonding with our dogs. And just those differences between baby talk and dog talk that Melson points out—the fact that we lower our voices, that we relax our expression, that we touch—show that there is a lot of research still to be done on the beautiful, complex, and, as of yet, mysterious way we communicate with our cherished dogs.

#1 QUIZ: PEE PROFILER

Your five-month-old puppy has a housebreaking mistake. You think:

a) Poor thing. He's teething, which I know from the *Veterinary Handbook* can throw off housebreaking, and I read on the Internet that the chewy I gave him may make pups extra thirsty.

b) I'll go mark that on his housebreaking chart on the fridge.

c) Damn it, should have closed the door to that room. This isn't rocket science!

d) Yup, pups go. What he probably needs is a good run.

e) He was frightened by that truck backfiring! Anything that sounds like gunfire terrifies him. He was probably abused by some man with a gun.

f) Oh, well, c'est la pee. Where's my odor neutralizer?

g) Arrrggghh! Why do you do these things to me? You are probably angry because I left. I came home late yesterday, you're just like my husband. . . .

h) Hmmm . . . I'll set an appointment up for the vet tomorrow to check for a urinary tract infection. It'll have to be in between my business lunch and picking the kids up at school.

i) I won't tolerate this. [At which point you drag the frightened pup over to the wet spot and let him have it—possibly ending with a spank or rubbing his face in it.]

j) Sorry pal . . . should have noticed you by the back door. I'll do better next time.

k) If that damn puppy mill hadn't kept him in a cage for those first four months, he'd be housebroken by now. The problem with dogs is people!

l) Actually, you don't notice any new wet spot amid all the dried wet spots.

a) Expert, b) Observer, c) Master, d) Buddy, e) Angel, f) Free Spirit, g) Projectionist end of Idealist, h) Dynamo, i) Warden end of Master, j) Soul Mate, k) Avenging Angel, l) Hoarding end of Angel

The Expert

Motto: Learning is love!

The Expert is a thoughtful person, which makes sense since the Expert is a Thinking type. She believes that answers to problems can be found through logical exploration of available information. Learning all there is to know about a dog (on the page, not the playing field) is the best way to ensure good care and a good outcome. Learning keeps the Expert and those she loves safe.

An evolved Expert couples brainpower—smart is a category trait and brilliance is not uncommon—with compassion. A good Expert is loving and loyal, and is often quite entertaining, with a wickedly sharp sense of humor.

The Expert is frequently the (or trying hard to be "the") serious dog person, the responsible one, the one in any group we would call earnest. Again, don't equate this term with humorless, because the Expert is often Class Wit (not to be confused with Class Clown). She tries hard to know the best food, best care, best collar, best trainers—exactly what's hot and what's not. There is no gossip that passes her by, no dog-related factoid she cannot recite.

Choosing her dog is a matter not just of the heart, but very much of the head. She would never just wake up one day, decide a dog is a good idea, and then skip down to the local shelter to pick out the "cutest one." The fact that the following is from a dog newbie underlines how Expert is an approach, not a destination:

And then I decided that given my lifestyle, a puppy was out of the question, and I should rescue an older dog. And I reasoned—if I'm going to get an older dog, I'd like a smart dog so I can train them. I had visions of a canine buddy that I could go hiking with and play fetch with—a companion, a pet I can spoil.

Right round this time, on successive weekends, I met two border collies. One of them belonged to a friend's houseguest at the beach—and when I went for a run early in the morning, Bronco decided to come with me. And decided he liked me that entire weekend. The second dog was a friend's dog that I taught to fetch the newspaper in like 10 minutes. So I thought—I have found my breed. Border collie.

I started doing research on the breed and read all the pros and cons of the breed. I read all the warnings . . .

How much more thorough could she be? For the record, after all that, she ended up with a dog who was a major challenge. That happens a lot, because dogs don't read.

Choosing a dog is just the beginning. When the puppy comes home, there's more research to be done. Along with study on food, crates, and breed-appropriate toys, Experts also fill dog classes for all sorts of training from agility to clicker, competition obedience to tracking. They are frequently the people who will have their dog in two divergent classes: a cutting-edge clicker class, perhaps, and a diametrically opposed old-school obedience class. It makes sense that the Expert explores both sides, because she is a sponge who wants to "learn it all." And, by the way: She wants to learn it all not to show off, but to provide the best for her pup and because she has an innate love of learning.

Since Experts are often more into "book learning" than hands-on practical knowledge, if they enter the organized world of dogs, they may gravitate toward roles like editor of their breed's newsletter. Though they may be disappointed in realizing that they can't know everything about breeding or showing or training, if they hang in there, embracing the "not knowing" of it all, they can become backbones in their breed or sport.

At their best, Experts are very connected to their dogs. "Learning" for the Expert includes getting to know her beloved companion as thoroughly as possible—not just which foods she should eat, or how much exercise she should get, but what makes her happy? Who is she? How does she signal that she's restless or hungry? How many words does she understand? The Expert finds joy in puzzling out her dog's emotions and character and personality. From the next room, the Expert can hear her dog drinking water and can gauge how empty or full the bowl is. She knows the second her dog isn't feeling well (though she may drive her vet crazy with both her fears and her armchair diagnosing). She reads her dog's expressions like . . . well, a book.

The Expert is often loyal to a breed and finds in that creature's face a gateway to a world beyond books and data. Experts in inanimate subjects may become brittle or rigid in their personal lives, but this is something that can't happen to an Expert on dogs. The dogs won't allow it. The throw-up on the rug, the unexpected behavior, the surprise lick across her glasses, all throw lovely monkey wrenches into the Expert's latest theory. Healthy Experts just LOVE that.

The Expert also has a strong sense of duty, and her dog will be walked no matter what the weather, her work schedule, or social pressures. If you head over to the park on a wintry day wondering if you will be alone, count on running into the Expert. Count on laughing for at

Wait, wait, don't interrupt me—I'm looking up "better ways to interact with your dog" in Wikipedia.

least a mile of that walk, too, though she may ask you if you've heard about this ointment that prevents snowballs from building up in your dog's pads.

Which leads us to the slippery slope for the Expert: the Know-It-All. If you've ever been harassed on a dog walk by someone determined to fire hose you with the contents of their burgeoning knowledge-reservoir, you've met one. How about those relentless, tireless opinionators on message boards and in chat rooms who have actually done little but say much? Let's face it: They're everywhere. They are info-bulimics.

In the dog world, they dish out big whopping ladles full of opinion (often nothing more than superstition and bad folk wisdom mixed with a little questionable Internet surfing). Most of what they "know" is tempered by very little actual hands-on experience. These people epitomize the great old line: "Frequently wrong but seldom in doubt." Fellow dog walkers at the park quickly learn how to avoid them, which means the Know-It-All increasingly circles within sight of the main gate, waiting for unsuspecting newcomers to pounce on. Instantly materializing, they call out, "Oh! You should try a gentle leader on your puppy!" as they dash over. Any unsuspecting novice owner with a young puppy is like chum to a great white shark for the Know-It-All.

The sometimes annoying but relatively harmless Know-It-All can degrade into the Expert's dark side: the "Right Fighter," who fights because the need to be "right" trumps everything else—compassion, evidence, friendship, peace, or health. While fear drives a lot of the Expert's zeal to understand and keep safe, the Right Fighters are harnessing their monsters—so flipped out about battling some threat (such as a propensity to cancer in the breed, perhaps) that they need to believe they've found the secret to beat it. Nothing, not even their own dog's ebbing health, can dissuade them.

Fortunately, these bad apple Experts are few and far between. The healthy and most common kind of Expert uses her knowledge to help others and make connections. Knowledge is power, and the Expert works diligently to acquire all the knowledge necessary to do the job of tending, training, and loving another species to the best of her abilities—an entirely admirable occupation. Experts are excellent people to hang around with, learn from,

LEAN ON ME

Dogs don't shoot us an "I knew you'd fail" look when we get fired. They don't sigh when we spend money we don't have on something we don't need. They don't walk out on us. They don't notice our potbellies, bad hair days, or cellulite. They lie down next to us in mansions or in cardboard boxes—protecting both equally. They wag a welcome to us when we are broke, homeless, or seriously dumped. And best of all, perhaps, no matter how harshly we judge ourselves, they never ever agree with our assessment. Dogs don't kick us when we're down; they lick us when we're down.

laugh with. And keep their phone numbers handy—you're going to want to call them in an emergency.

You May Be an Expert If You:

- Know all about the latest pet product recalls.
- Have taken one or more dog-training classes.
- Carry a clicker.
- Have memorized the "best" veterinary handbook, can recommend the best local vets, and have the stories to tell about the others.
- Are the responsible dog owner and want everyone else to be one, too.
- Can list the first five ingredients in most dog foods.

- Use the word "bitch" in casual conversation: *Your bitch has a great rear.*
- Discuss the graphic details of skin diseases, fecal formation, and wound infection in loud tones at public restaurants without a second thought. The often-misheard topic of anal sacs is a biggie.
- Provide a better diet and health care for your dog than yourself.
- Have multiple dog beds placed near your computer, bed, TV, and in at least one corner of the kitchen.

You're *Not* a True Expert If You:

- Have ever bought your dog food from the supermarket. A true "Expert" will clutch her chest when she reads that line. "SUPERMARKET—who gets food from a SUPER-MARKET?! Do you know what's in that stuff? . . ." And, in an attempt to limit letters from Experts and subscribers to *Whole Dog Journal*, this is not a comment on what food is best for your dog. That is a decision each person should make for themselves with as much self-education as possible. There are many great foods available today, but rest assured of one thing—no matter what you feed, some will support you 100 percent and others will not (usually passionately, too frequently impolitely—and expect to hear how what you are doing will "kill your dog"). Welcome to what we have come to call "The Dog Food Wars."
- Go to the same veterinarian for many years because he's convenient and "good enough."
- Can ignore that rambunctious terrier mix who's starting a fight, again!
- Think a "bait bag" is some kind of fishing gear.

You May Be Headed for Trouble If:

- You notice people get quiet when you walk up, and some drift away.
- Sighing, your vet pulls out his biggest, heaviest manuals to show you why it's not necessary to test for Cushing's disease (again).
- People's usual responses to your comments are things like: "oh," "um," "really?"
- You get booted off one or more message boards (and you're *definitely* a "Know-It-All" if you think that happens because others are "jealous of" or "threatened by" all you know).

Favorite Names

Frequently based on breed research and often involves hard-to-pronounce but geographically appropriate monikers: Misniuil, Goethe, or Paikea. If the dog's name has to be explained to you, it's probably an Expert's dog. *"I named him Jackson after Jackson Pollock because of his merle patches—isn't that a scream?"*

Sweet Nothings

When he's praised, the Expert's dog will be told how smart he is—possibly in two or three languages. Or how perfectly designed—Vicki's wolfhound Tally is nicknamed Taliesin (Frank Lloyd Wright's estate) because of her great "architecture."

Tips for Training

You may start off as an aficionado of a certain approach, doing that and just that, but as you go along, as you read, you'll try things, you'll try something else, you'll stick with some trainers, try others, attend seminars, and then talk about how you sort of do X's method but with

a little Y thrown in because that just makes sense to you. (The fact that you can converse on various trainers' methods sooooo makes you an Expert.)

Character-Building Exercises

- For one week: Read no dog books or magazines. Instead, watch your dog—he's the real expert on dog behavior! (And once you get used to it, try it on a regular basis.)
- Hire . . . (gulp) . . . an animal communicator.
- Next time you hear a question about dogs at the park—don't answer it.

Breeds to Which Experts Are Drawn

Experts are often breed loyalists, either polygamous or serially monogamous with "their" breed. Many are drawn to the quieter, less intrusive breeds, as these dogs are not as prone to interrupting their train of thought or marathon reading jags. Such dogs would include most of the sight hounds (greyhounds, Borzoi, Saluki, Irish Wolfhounds), the Chow, a Pekingese. If in the mood, Experts can handle extreme grooming requirements, enjoying both the effort and the result—so Afghans, Poodles, Bichons, Lhasa Apsos, or Soft-Coated Wheatens in full glory might be favorites. In general, they need to avoid reading books about rare breeds, or else they might become intrigued by some that look great in glossy photos and have interesting histories, but would be terrible for their lifestyle, such as the New Guinea Singing Dog or Thai Ridgeback.

Breeds Experts Should Avoid

Breeds whose independent behavior will make the Expert look like a rank amateur: Miniature Pinschers, Finnish Spitz, Siberian Huskies, or any other breed known for its mischievous personality.

The Expert in Love

SOUL MATE—Probably not, even if the Expert has a little dash of Soul Mate in his or her makeup. The Expert tries to be analytical, to take more of an intellectual approach to dog ownership for the good of the dog; the Soul Mate believes all answers come from the heart. And the term "ownership"? How utterly crass. That sounds uncomfortably reminiscent of the slave trade. The Soul Mate is a "guardian" and doesn't give a darn about what that means legally—she just wants everyone to know how much (and how well) she loves her dogs.

EXPERT—Expert squared. If you agree with each other, then this could work, but what two Experts agree with each other?

DYNAMO—Possible, as long as the Expert has other people around to educate. The Dynamo doesn't really have time to sit still for lectures and briefings. Add it to the list or move aside—the Dynamo's got things to do!

ANGEL—Maybe, if the Expert is supportive of the Angel's work and the Angel can lean on the Expert for information and guidance. In that case, this is a pair that could open a rescue operation together. Experts may like Angels as friends, but it's harder to make it work in a love pairing.

IDEALIST—The relationship could run a tad dry for each, but there are possibilities. Both types care about getting things right, and as a team, they could fire on two rockets.

MASTER—Absolutely, as long as both are at the same level of expertise. The Expert can be reading the most recent publications while the Master is out trying the newest techniques.

LUXURY PET CARE: A NEW TREND?

Doggy daycare, fat camp for dogs, canine massage, physical therapy—when will this modern-day indulgence-fest end? Who knows? But we can tell you when it may have begun—sometime in the 1870s. That's when this article appeared in a book about dogs of the British Isles:

> *An ex-kennelman in our neighborhood made a very comfortable income by this peculiar practice [taking weight off fat dogs]. When I fetched 'em from their mistresses they refused to eat what I should have been glad to get, and when they went back they would eat what I couldn't touch. I've had some dogs twice or three times a year, but I always cured them at last. One of them was as good as three pounds a year[1] to me. I was terrible fond of him, but he never took to me; when he saw me coming for him to bring down his fat, he would waddle away and howl enough to wake the dead.[2]*

So the next time someone huffs about how our dogs are indulged like never before, and how our society-gone-mad spends money on "ridiculous" luxury services, you can reply with confidence that, in fact, this is nothing new. We pet people have been paying for "ridiculous" luxury services for 135 years . . . at least.

1   Which translates to around $2,700 in today's dollars, http://eh.net/hmit/.

2   *Dogs of the British Islands, A Series of Articles and Letters by Various Contributors,* edited by "Stonehenge," London 1872, chapter 12: Ancient and Modern Toy Dogs.

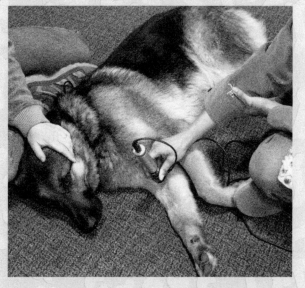

Sarah's dog gets physical therapy. Over the top? Not to us!

FREE SPIRIT—Counterintuitively, this can work if the Expert wants someone to help her occasionally tiptoe out of her comfort zone and if the Free Spirit craves just a little structure. That's not to say that this is one of those "we never fight!" relationships—in fact, it could ratchet up from The Bickersons to The Battlesons fast. But it could also be a lot of fun.

OBSERVER—This sounds sweet: Someone who likes to learn meets someone who needs to teach. It can work in a friendship, but on the romantic level, the Observer is a little too self-contained for an Expert who craves feedback, and the Expert is a little too intrusive for an Observer.

BUDDY—A big yawn from both corners. The Expert has some admiration for the Buddy's easy knowledge of portable camp stoves and tent placement in relation to wind direction, but the bottom line is that she really doesn't like to go camping. The Buddy could get into having someone around who actually *reads* instructions, but after that, then what? If this relationship starts, the end won't be dramatic—the Expert just won't answer the calls that the Buddy isn't bothering to make.

#2 QUIZ: THE PUPPY RESPONSE

You see a four-month-old puppy on the sidewalk ahead of you. . . .

a) You walk by. After all, the pup may be in training and you don't want to mess that up.

b) You smile instantly and greet the owners, asking about their new charge.

c) You whip out a treat and start to explain to the owner how to lure their puppy into a sit.

d) You pause for a few moments to watch the pup interact with someone else.

e) You greet the person, then squat down to say hello to the pup, using one hand to keep the pup from leaping up on you.

f) You squat down, speaking excitedly and rubbing his head back and forth, laughing as the pup leaps at your face.

g) You greet the pup and the person briefly, then get on with your day.

h) You squat down, quietly cooing to the pup, who submissively pees on you, but you don't mind.

i) You smile at the owner as you rough up the pup for a few seconds before continuing on your run.

a) Master, b) Soul Mate, c) Expert, d) Observer, e) Idealist, f) Free Spirit, g) Dynamo, h) Angel, i) Buddy

The Dynamo

Motto: Just do it!

This Dogology personality type materialized from the oh-so-modern affliction of a lack of time the way Athena sprang forth from Zeus. We all have more to do than we have time to do it in, but it is the Dynamo who gets to doing. Like the Marines, the Dynamo gets more done before 9:00 a.m. than most of us get done in a day. These Energizer Bunnies have excellent focus and an admirable ability to complete tasks. They are the very reason for the adage, "If you want something done, ask a busy person," which points to the truth: Dynamos do and do it well.

Often these people are working parents with a lot on their plates. They simply don't have time for dysfunction—the laundry needs doing, the kids have to be dropped off or picked up, dinner must be made, life goes on . . . and on . . . and on. They understand the choices they've made and the obligations they've taken on. These are not the folks who buy a Saint Bernard and then call a trainer to bemoan the fact that the dog got so large. Nor are they the ones who get an Old English Sheepdog just to let it get dirty and matted. If they take on a responsibility, they know what they are taking on and follow through, all the way.

Because love is expressed through doing, most dogs (and kids for that matter) in these homes are well-fed, clean, fairly well groomed, have playdates, see the doctor right on schedule, and are amply educated—but all may be a tad short on tender hugs and quiet together time.

In the Dynamo's world, she may be the least hounded by her hound, who offers the most consistent and least demanding emotional support she gets, and in return, the hound gets some of the attention and physical affection other people in her life may crave. People who know her in her career or outside the home may be floored when they see the gentle, unself-conscious caresses and geyser of baby talk directed toward the dog. This is great news for a dog, who can get the very best this person has to offer.

Once the Dynamo puts dog walking or a visit to the park on the daily list of to-dos, it will be adhered to religiously. (The Dynamo may thoroughly enjoy this mandated fun, relishing the relatively slow time for park people interactions and quiet immersion in nature.) Training is the same. The Dynamo will do it and do it as instructed. She may not be able to improvise or combine methods when the need arises, which can lead to frustration as, again, she's doing the very best she can and exactly as instructed.

It may seem odd, but more than one Dynamo's dog we know could use some time with Jenny Craig. We suspect that all people have to slow down sometime, and when the kids are in bed, the kitchen is clean, and the next day is planned out, the Dynamo and her dog may sit down for a heart-to-heart with Pepperidge Farm. A little shared carbo-loading slows the human down while rounding out the dog. The Dynamo may deny it to your face, but the dog's waistline doesn't lie.

A Dynamo is in such constant motion that he or she is practically a blur whipping through life with a much-beloved dog often riding shotgun. A touchstone in a hectic day, the dog can bring a smile, calming a tense owner with a glance upward and a few wags. Here a Dynamo takes time to tell us of this connection:

They are always happy to see me and offer me a "groundedness" during a busy day. They are soothing to me and force me to keep my priorities straight and not get so busy with work and achieving that I forget about the simple pleasures in life.

The dogs are clearly loved—for what they offer the Dynamo—soothing to *me*, keeping *my* priorities straight, so *I* don't forget. This points to a Dynamo risk: She can do so much for so many that she always feels like she's running on empty, and then everything can become about the Dynamo's needs, not so much about the loved ones. When that happens, she can become the inner hip boot–wearing, whip-toting Multitasker for whom doing many things at once is a belief system. Who has time to do "just" one thing? So the dog's bowl is put down, while she's on the phone, the dinner is in the microwave, and the evening news is on. The Multitasker is just too busy to truly enjoy her own life, never mind share herself with the dog or her kids or her friends. Nothing gets done with attention or awareness, but by the end of the day, she has a long list of comforting accomplishments to tumble into bed with (where she is way too tired to be comforted by much else).

If you listen hard when speaking to a serious Multitasker, you may hear what lies farther down this slippery slope: the squeaking of the inner hamster running endlessly on her own wheel. These people are busy, not because they have a lot to do (which they always do) but because that's how they like their life and want to live it. For them, doing—being constantly on the move—seems to prove both their value and their importance. They possess a dog because, in theory, they like what a dog represents—a "complete" life—but they like the image more than the reality. They go to the park just so they can check "walked the dog" off in their leather-bound day-planner. They consider that time to be "wasted" if they aren't on their cell phone or BlackBerry taking care of more "important" things. No matter what they are doing, the thing they aren't doing is "more important."

If she isn't careful, she can end up with a lifelong list of tasks, but no actual life. Relationships—with people or dogs—take time and openness, meaning first you have to make the time and then you have to make the room. Many reasons can lurk below this life-style—you might feel that no one could possibly love you for who you are, only for what you do; another is that by doing a lot, you are worth a lot, or possibly you're from a long line of such "hard workers" and this is the life model you have internalized. Whatever the source, you need to know that doing isn't the same as loving (no matter what you've been told), so be careful.

Dynamos tend to be the envy of their friends, efficiently running their lives while juggling the many demands of today's world. Most of us could use a healthy dose of Dynamo (along with a few more hours to sleep). Few stray into the manic world of Multitasking; rather they adore their families through the act of taking care of them in tangible and measurable ways. It is a lucky dog who finds himself curled up next to a Dynamo as she composes her list for the day. Every one of his needs will be on that list, rest assured.

You May Be a Dynamo If You:

- Have the dog walker on speed dial.
- Use (and love) doggy daycare because that alleviates much of your guilt about not having more time. The dog comes home exhausted—perfection!
- Go to the park in the suit you wore to work.
- Walk your dog alone or maybe with one friend.
- Don't take time to train the dog, but expect the dog to be obedient and "understand."
- Have talked to others at the park often, but never remember anyone's name.
- Would rather text-message or e-mail someone than talk to them directly.
- Have a couple of crates that you use to park the dog, the way some parents park their kids in front of the TV.

Dynamos? If yes, then they are killing three birds with one stone (walk dog, walk self, catch up with friend).

You're *Not* a True Dynamo If You Have:

- Ever sat on a bench in the park.
- Ever taken an extra lap around the park just to listen to a friend.
- Ever left your cell phone at home.

- Ever laughed while in the park with your dog (unrelated to cell phone use).
- Dirty dishes in your sink right now.

You May Be Headed for Trouble If:

- You have not played with your dog (or your kids) within the last two weeks.
- Talking to human beings seems like a waste of precious time.
- You can't remember the last time you sat on the floor and played with your dog.

Favorite Names

Ones that probably have been Googled off the most popular baby names list from the decade the Dynamo was born. Human names such as Ben or Sally are selected because the Dynamo, whether she realizes it or not, wants a friend.

Sweet Nothings

When he's praised, the Dynamo's dog will hear what a nice dog he is—that he is no trouble at all. Sometimes there will be a grinning, teasing patter—"What a pain in the &** you are! Whose idea were you? Like I have time for you!"—all spoken lovingly as the Dynamo rubs the dog's chest and the dog's tail thumps happily.

Tips for Training

Is there a speed-training course out there? Fifteen minutes to the perfect dog? No? Too bad. In that case you'll get to the most popular class in the area and go religiously. Once it's in your schedule, it gets done.

Character-Building Exercises

- Lie in the sun with your dog—aim for at least ten minutes, but we'd settle for five.
- Go to the park with no agenda and just watch the dogs.
- Take a nap—we dare you.

Breeds to Which Dynamos Are Drawn

Soft-Coated Wheaten Terriers, Portuguese Water Dogs, and other nonshedders, as well as Jack Russell Terriers (or Parson Russell or whatever they are being called these days). But that's not who they *should* want. They should want a calm, stable dog who is happy to just "come along for the ride" as the Dynamo whizzes through her day. A nice calm Labrador or laid-back Cavalier gets our tail-thumping approval.

Breeds Dynamos Should Avoid

Anxious or reactive breeds who need a hands-on, emotional connection to feel comfortable, such as Shetland Sheepdogs. A Portuguese Water Dog, Jack Russell, or Australian Shepherd may spin out of control in this hectic home—refracting the owner's energy into chaos. A sensitive Italian Greyhound or Chihuahua may spend all too much time shaking under a table, and besides, they are vulnerable to being squashed by the big feet of people focused on moving forward.

The Dynamo in Love

SOUL MATE—Maybe, if the Dynamo doesn't try to intrude on the Soul Mate's relation-ship with her dog (and any contact with the dog may be seen as intruding if you have an

extreme Soul Mate on your hands). But since the Dynamo's need for comfort and connection may also be extreme and emotionally subterranean, that is unlikely. If both bring dogs into the relationship, things may work out better.

EXPERT—Possible match if their priorities align and the Dynamo is willing to add the Expert's suggestions to his or her list. The Dynamo may enjoy the Expert's knowledge, and the Expert may appreciate the Dynamo's competence.

DYNAMO—Double Dynamo. Here are two ships in the night, only real ships in the night probably see more of each other than would two Dynamos. If these two set up date nights and a regular schedule for sex, things could work. Otherwise neither will get done and both will feel like what they are—lonely (and no one likes to feel that way).

ANGEL—Not likely. Angels can be chaotic and messy, two things that drive a solid Dynamo to distraction.

IDEALIST—Near-perfect match; the Dynamo likes to do the right thing in the right order, and the Idealist likes things to be done right and right away. The Right family.

MASTER—Maybe . . . if the Dynamo will use her powers for good, helping the Master send in entry forms on time and pack the van for a weekend of agility trials, and if the Master picks up the training and exercising of the dog, which checks two things off the Dynamo's Sisyphean list, this could work.

FREE SPIRIT—This is Mother Loosey Goosey meets Father Stay-on-Time—there's gonna be trouble. The Dynamo will be accused of being "anal retentive" and "inflexible," and the Free Spirit will hear words like "flaky" and "immature." Unless that scenario appeals (and it does for some people), they should skip it. Advice to each: Save the money you would have spent on flowers and dinner and spring for a session with a really good therapist, because honestly, what were you thinking?

OBSERVER—Absolutely. The Dynamo will "do," and the Observer will notice and applaud. Both will feel great about themselves and each other, and neither will notice the emotional limitations of these two types: perfection!

BUDDY—Potentially combustible combo—while the Dynamo wants to use Saturday to get things done (run to the pet store, drop the pup off at the groomer's for a quick bath, race to the vet to pick up those ear meds), the Buddy wants to be off hiking with the dog through a gorgeous local swamp. The Buddy's zest for life can appeal mightily to the Dynamo, who might just use the Buddy for a little casual sex or will, at the very least, fantasize about it.

#3 QUIZ: THE SECRETS OF PLAY

Your favorite game to play with your dog is:

a) My trainer says to blend work with play and play with work, so instead of games, I have her practice polite behaviors.

b) I'm thinking of getting an automatic tennis ball tosser. My dog will love it, and I can get other things done . . .

c) Game? Training, of course!

d) I love it when she grabs a sock and I chase her around the house, that's the best.

e) We love to do tricks together; we have the best time!

f) The best games to play with a dog of this breed and age are ones that focus on control and cooperation. So many people just let their dogs run wild, which isn't smart. I just read a book that outlines this phenomenon in detail, it's called . . .

g) Game? He just crashes after our hikes.

h) I hide things for him to find. He loves that, and I love to watch him figure things out.

i) I hold her in my lap and rock her and tell her how much I love her and how special she is, and she falls asleep in my arms. . . . I love that.

a) Idealist, b) Dynamo, c) Master, d) Free Spirit, e) Soul Mate, f) Know-It-All end of Expert, g) Buddy, h) Observer, i) Angel

The Angel

Motto: Love conquers all!

Angels adopt/rescue dogs, offering them safe, permanent shelter, volunteer for needy causes, and are the consciences of society. We should be throwing rose petals in the path of these tender Feeler types because they see the beauty in the sickest, smallest, skinniest, shyest of dogs. More than one of her dogs may be one-eyed or three-legged or both. Another in the pack may be seen sporting doggy diapers and wheeling his paralyzed back end around in a custom cart. In fact, for many Angels, a "special needs" dog has more appeal than a best-in-show model. Wow! The world needs more Angels!

You might not always recognize the ones who are out there, since plenty of them are camouflaged. Often limited by a spouse who doesn't want to have their home turned into a farm, some Angels become Angels of moderation. They have one or two dogs. Because their dog gathering has been curtailed, they might supplement the pet count with smaller, less noticeable creatures such as rabbits, cats, birds, rats, and gerbils. (If an Angel has kids, you'll know her by the van-load of other people's children she picks up with her own every day from school.)

When Angels choose dogs who are sweet-tempered and basically self-disciplining (such as a roly-poly Lab or two), their houses run smoothly. And their home is always a place everyone else's dogs enjoy visiting. Just as your grandmother did with you, the Angel will not let a visiting pooch leave without being stuffed with some special delight: Snausages, chewies, and a few organic goodies from the local "barkery."

As the Angel's dogs get older and roly-polier, count on seeing the addition of helpful gear: a stowaway ramp for the car, orthopedic beds all over the floor, and a midriff sling to haul him up and down the stairs (even though the dog may outweigh the Angel). This is the Angel of mercy.

If the Angel doesn't have self-disciplining dogs, animal behavior may be baffling for her—because, in her world, love and understanding are supposed to cure all. She's not into any training that uses "force," and a tenderhearted Angel can interpret "force" as almost every kind of command—the Angel doesn't want to exert her will over the poor animal; she wants the dog to want to behave. (One Angel we know carefully drove the mile back to her house from the park with her terrier trotting beside the car—his leash out the driver's side window. Why? Because he would not relinquish the oozing carcass he had picked up.) This obviously isn't the most effective training approach, but that's okay by this type. Angels aren't about a quick fix—they believe in love and time. Angels cope by showing epic patience. They are willing to work on some small bit of behavior for months rather than accepting tougher short-cuts.

The Angel is attracted to the wounded and the suffering. She is a kind of Lourdes for Labradors. The maimed, the matted, the mangy will beat a path to her open door. She has a sixth sense for finding dogs who have been abused by their previous owners (though she may sometimes read abuse into a history where there has been none). Here is classic Angel commentary:

My dog is always upbeat and cheery. Her zest for life is inspirational, since she was a rescued dog from abuse. Her true, hidden personality has emerged even though it took time. She went from an angry, scared, aggressive dog to one whose temperament has done a 180-degree turnaround with understanding, love, and training. She doesn't need spoken language to communicate. Her humor, her wit, her love has endeared her to us and our other animals. She shares the house with three cats who are older than her (she's three) but who accepted her and she them. In fact, we call her "Big Kitty" sometimes because she wants to be one of them.

What are the giveaways that this is an Angel talking? The enthusiasm and wonder evident in the description of the animal and the perception that the dog's "true personality" has been hidden by prior abuse. Through understanding and love, all is revealed, and to a warm, welcoming, and loving Angel, what is revealed is perfect: a resurrection story with passion and glory. In that short paragraph, we learn the dog is upbeat, cheery, zest-filled, inspirational, humorous, witty, plays well with others, and is a good communicator. Pretty sweet, and hard to imagine a prouder parent than that!

Angels often take great joy in their dogs' playful and even naughty antics, which they see not as "problems," but as proof that the dog feels safe and secure in their care. And behaviors that *are* problems, such as poor housebreaking, are seen as side effects of the past abuse or neglect and "not the dog's fault."

You're getting the message by now: The Angel may not be the best teacher, trainer, or taskmaster. But you know what? Who cares? Not the Angel. And not anyone who loves and appreciates the Angel. She doesn't mind cleaning up the pee, throwing away the chewed shoes, or filling in the backyard holes; she even *enjoys* it because providing a safe environment for her dogs that is free of negativity is her happiness.

Acts of affection—petting, talking to, cradling in her lap (even with absurdly large dogs)— are offered so often that sometimes it's even more than the dog wants. Because of her drive to be loving, kind, and sweet, an Angel might not even notice that the dog is turning away from her. If she does, she'll laugh, pulling his head around for yet one more kiss on the nose. *He's such a big silly, Mommy loves him!*

The world is a better place because of Angels, and many, many dogs owe their lives to them. It is unadulterated joy to see an Angel immersed in loving what is almost always a delightfully happy gaggle of misfits. It gives you faith in humanity.

What some Angels need to be on guard against is that it's not always a long walk to their slippery slope, where the Angel develops an inverse relationship between how much dogs are loved with how much people are disliked. "People" are seen as the bad guys, the abusers of animals. And the Angel is wearing the white hat. She is the one who saves those animals from suffering. Here's a voice from someone starting to slide down that slippery slope:

Our three house dogs are also all rescued dogs. Only one is a purebred—a Basenji who was a stray and ended up in a shelter. Dogs are more wonderful than humans for the most part. They love you no matter what. And if you are feeling bad, be it physically, mentally, or emotionally, they are always there by your side, giving you sympathy and love.

Once this seed has sprouted, the "Avenging Angel" may well be born. She wants to save all the dogs—that includes your dog from you and all dogs from everyone else, too. In her mind, *no one* cares for animals as much as or as well as she does. That is a point of great pride and profound sense of moral superiority. Listen carefully for the clues in her comments: how she could *never* buy a dog when so many are being "murdered"—her term—in shelters every day; how she would *never* use X or Y piece of training equipment because it's "so mean" (as her dogs drag themselves on lead until they are gagging); that she would *never* go to a groomer/ use a kennel/hire a dog walker—because she's heard what "those people" do.

She may well volunteer at the local shelter, but soon she's at war with the staff there about which dogs are not safe and which ones deserve another chance. From there she starts bending the group's rules because she thinks she knows better.

If she doesn't get help, she could end up on the dark side of Angel, where dogs are hoarded (collected). These are the folks behind the headline "Local Shelter Raids

BABY DOG

This picture illustrates why we are helpless when it comes to dogs. The beagle is relaxed and blissful in this person's lap—cradled like a baby, looking up and making eye contact.

Someone puts an upward-facing, small, warm, relaxed, happy being in your arms, and your heart thuds gratefully against your rib cage. It is a miracle of connection.

Notice what you do and what you feel when you have a dog in this position—do you rock him a bit, dive straight into baby talk, cuddle him closer, gaze into his eyes? Of course you do, because, thankfully, that is what we are hardwired to do. And does the dog sigh in pure joy, wag his tail, flop in your arms, and gaze up into your face? Of course he does, because, even more thankfully, yes, that's what he is hardwired to do. It works for us. It works for both of us. We are both wired for love.

Trailer—Finds 105 Dogs." What investigators are discovering is that this kind of mental illness is frequently a response to previous abuse[1] and that the hoarder seems to believe that as long as no one is beating, screaming at, or actively harming the animals, then all is well. Maybe these souls are trying to save themselves over and over again in a *Groundhog Day*–like loop in which the absence of the sort of harm that harmed them equals a good life.

---

1   http://lib.bioinfo.pl/pmid:17673166

The hoarder trusts no one to keep "her babies" safe (76 percent of hoarders are women). So the animals start to add up. The dogs in such care may live their lives in crates or pens; they may breed, never get outside, and never receive adequate vet care, but the hoarder cannot see any of that. All she can see is that she is offering kindness.

Such tragic cases make up a tiny percentage of this stellar type. They should never be seen as representing the true Angel, who is a vital force for the welfare of animals. Whether it is her own beloved brood or animals in a larger sense, dogs could have no one better in their corner than a passionate, compassionate Angel.

You May Be an Angel If You:

- Always have a dog with a story—the one who was tossed from a car, was chained to a tree, is blind, or couldn't find a home because he had no bladder control.
- Have more than one dog because how can you turn down this other needy one?
- Become incensed if you spot an intact male dog. You cannot leave without a lecture on neutering or an over-the-shoulder remark like, *"Hey, we're not talking about YOURS."* (But you kinda are . . .)
- Clean up all dog poop at the park—your dog's, other dogs', whatever. It needs to be picked up, right?
- Tear up when you watch the ASPCA or North Shore ads on Animal Planet (which is your favorite channel). You send money whenever you can.
- Carry your ancient, blind, incontinent, confused, immobile dog in and out four times a day to potty.
- Lie awake at night worrying about all the animals that need help.

You're *Not* a True Angel If You:

- Ever think, "Oh, that dog isn't so cute."
- Know that some dogs just aren't good pets.
- Pass by a dog without making cooing noises to him.
- Greet the humans before you greet their dogs.
- Decide to send your donations for scholarships this year.

You May Be Headed for Trouble If:

- There is *any* dried feces or urine inside your house.
- Any one of your dogs has not seen a vet for more than a year.
- You become enraged if anyone suggests you should re-home any of your growing number of animals.
- You're a member of a militant animal rights group and treat it as an evangelical religion.
- *You have ever* left a hateful voice mail message regarding dogs or flamed some newbie on the Petfinder message boards.

Favorite Names

Anything that evokes rising from nothingness to greatness: Phoenix, Oprah, Annie (as in Li'l Orphan). Anything that speaks of home as a haven: Dorothy (there's no place like home). Or names that celebrate dogs as permanently infantile, such as Baby or Puppy.

Sweet Nothings

When he's praised, the Angel's dog will hear how special he is, how he's loved "just the way" he is, how he will always be loved, how he is safe, how the Angel will never hurt him, how no one will hurt him again . . .

Tips for Training

You support, advocate, and believe completely in "all-positive" training, so grab a clicker and get clicking. You'll have a blast building behaviors both you and your dog enjoy. This is a growing niche in the training market, and you can find plenty of books and resources about clicker training on the Internet.

Character-Building Exercises

- Just once, don't jump up the second one of the dogs barks at the cookie jar.
- Go to a local shelter and just notice everything good they are doing (more of a challenge: don't come home with anyone new).
- Ask the opinion of someone you trust (and who will tell you honestly) about how you are caring for your dogs, then listen.

Breeds to Which Angels Are Drawn

Whichever dog is listed as "On Death Row" at the local shelter. Angels are admirably open-minded; breed and mix are simply irrelevant to an Angel, who understands that they all need love.

Breeds Angels Should Avoid

Since a house full of untrained dogs is the Angel norm, breeds and individual dogs that tend to fight with other dogs should be resisted: many terriers, Akitas (for which dog aggression is expected by AKC standard), and other powerful dogs with six-shooters tucked in their belts. There are so many sweet, needy dogs out there just waiting for you—don't let them down!

The Angel in Love

SOUL MATE—A Soul Mate who is willing to love more than one dog at a time has a chance with the Angel. The risk here is that a quiet war of attachment can erupt with "whom does the dog like better?" Avoid this pitfall, and the dogs in the home will be intensely cherished.

EXPERT—These two stand a chance of bringing out the best in each other. The Angel softens the Expert, and the Expert gives structure to the Angel. Working together, they can raise a happy, healthy little menagerie.

DYNAMO—Not too likely. Angels want to do the helping; they generally don't want others trying to help them too much. And the Dynamo whizzing around can make anyone feel judged—the Angel is no exception—even though the Dynamo may not be judging anyone but themselves.

ANGEL—Angel squared. Maybe, in the beginning, where they can save dogs together— and together much good can be done. From there, though, things have the potential to morph into "you and me against the world" thinking. When that's comfortable and

Angels love their dogs deeply, but may share poorly. ➤

fun—fine. But just don't take it too far, where the risk becomes tumbling into isolationist, down-with-people thinking.

IDEALIST—In the Angel's opinion, this can work, but only as a serious spiritual makeover project. She (and Angels are generally women) believes that (like every other pet she's taken in) the Idealist just needs a lot of love to bloom. The Idealist may just respect the purity of this woman's heart. But he needs to tread carefully; the Angel is supportive and loving only as long as one agrees with her pet-care choices. Disagree and a partner may find the sharp-clawed cat lurking inside that kitten. She will protect her charges!

MASTER—We don't think so. Angel views Master as someone with control issues who needs to stay well back from her fur-babies. For her, any Master verges on an abuser who doesn't "love the animals for themselves." And for the Master's part, the Angel only gives what she wants to give, not what the dog needs, so she's a form of abuser. Don't even sit them next to each other at a dinner party, never mind try to get them into bed!

FREE SPIRIT—Here we go! No hurtful words, no limit to love. The only disagreement might be over whether to get just one more dog or two. This is a love nest!

OBSERVER—Could work if the Observer is verging on being a bystander who can dispassionately watch the goings-on with little comment other than support. His cerebral aloofness might actually help the Angel steady herself.

BUDDY—Not likely, since the Buddy's casual approach to leashes and safety will give an Angel even more of those nightmares she experiences all too often as it is (full of speeding pickup trucks with cute puppies riding loose in back).

#4 QUIZ: WITNESS FOR THE DEFENSE OR PROSECUTION?

You are walking in the park and see a young woman with a rambunctious Golden Retriever on a retractable lead. The dog spots a squirrel and lunges, pulling the woman down to the ground. You think:

a) The dog needs some exercise!

b) That was totally preventable with some basic leash work.

c) Gosh, that happened to me, just last week!

d) What a happy, enthusiastic dog—she's obviously full of life!

e) That looked painful. I don't think those leads look safe.

f) Ouch! Getting hurt would mess up my whole week. I'm going to toss my retractable lead.

g) How embarrassing! I hope she didn't rip that lovely jacket she's got on.

h) Oh, she must be so upset! The dog didn't mean it; he just wanted to have some fun.

i) If she had started training when she should have and gone to a good puppy kindergarten, this would never have happened. These sorts of accidents are totally preventable if people would just get as much information about the dogs they are going to have for ten or more years as they get about buying a dishwasher.

a) Buddy, b) Master, c) Free Spirit, d) Angel, e) Observer, f) Dynamo, g) Idealist, h) Soul Mate, i) Expert

The Idealist

Motto: Do it right!

There is a right way to do things, so why would you do them any other way? The Idealist has high standards for herself, and though she knows that's not the case for everybody, people's failure to do what is obvious can be a little incomprehensible to her. The Idealist is the workhorse of any group activity, quietly making sure every yard sale item is priced properly or that all the brownies have been cut into perfect squares. If the local dog park needs anything, the Idealist will be at the helm steering the project from the idea stage through the red tape to completion. Idealists are the precious 10 percent of any group who actually show up consistently and do more than complain. They are reliable, strong, and steady.

They like their home to look like a home; things mostly match—from dish towels to back-splashes to curtains. The most warmhearted of this type make the very greatest of friends. They are there for you in a crisis, they give rock-solid advice, and they encourage you to strive for the best within yourself.

And so it is in their relationships with their dogs. The Idealist researches the right breed, picks up a dog bed that matches the decor, buys a few top puppy-rearing books, interviews a veterinarian or two (even though one of them was recommended by a close friend), and signs up for the top local puppy training class before exiting the breeder's driveway (or had it book-marked). Generally thorough, prepared, punctual, honest, and true—the Idealist is basically a Boy or Girl Scout. A puppy may (happily) add a little chaos and humor to this life:

Bones has changed our lives—we are amazed at how devoted we are to him (and he is to us) and how much joy he brings us. Our friends are shocked that we (who were neat freaks and unencumbered by kids) allow Bones to jump onto the bed and couches, drag in twigs and leaves, etc. We've just loosened up.

You can just hear the happiness in this Idealist's voice. What a delightful and lucky dog Bones must be—to be so adored for being himself.

A happy, evolved Idealist provides a loving as well as practical home for a dog. Praise doesn't come cheap in this household—dogs (and kids) must earn it. But it feels very good when it is received. Warm, judicious Idealists make ideal parents and/or dog owners. Expectations are high, but realistic, and everyone knows where they stand and what the rules are. Part of establishing those rules is a basic, underlying understanding of dogdom. Idealists tend to know their stuff and work hard to educate themselves.

The compensation to each is terrific: A dog gets structure, consistency, and love, and the Idealist (who can be so hard on himself/herself) gains an ally for his or her soul. The dog is forgiving, bright, and may just persuade the Idealist—at least sometimes—to cut himself or herself a little slack. An Idealist with a true-blue dog may even learn to be a little less self-critical—a gift she really deserves. What the Idealist already has in his or her arsenal is the ability to be consistent and judicious. Combined with love and kindness, these two characteristics allow a dog to really bloom. Many of us have witnessed that a dog is never so proud as when doing a job right. The Idealist makes sure this happens. She helps her dog learn and work—and when the dog performs, he truly revels in the approval of his owner. The pairing of an Idealist with a dog can be a thing of trust and beauty: a team with a deep, secure bond. That's the best end of the spectrum.

The Idealist's slippery slope, that place where qualities suddenly shift from admirable to uh-oh? That would be the Image Maker. Celebutantes and proponents of pit bull–fighting coexist in this ego swamp where dogs exist to serve the image of the owner. Image Makers hate visible flaws; perfection (however they personally define it) is the goal.

Whether wearing a dog on her arm as others might swing a purse or sporting a rippling-muscled dog's aggression as a fashion statement, the Image Maker is using a dog to say, "See who I am, see what I am about." Of course, to a certain extent, we all do this. We select breeds or mixes that we are attracted to for some reason—that speak for some part of us. The dividing line is when people harm or neglect the animal (even "a little") as they do so—then the "attachment" rings hollow.

Hollow begins when a dog becomes a fashion accessory. Many Idealists who slide down that slippery slope to become Image Makers have grown up in a situation where possessions reflected a person's value, gifts were labeled as love, and appearance was everything. So, no shocker, the dog is loved for how he makes this Image Maker look.

On the violent or macho side of this slope, the dog is still an accessory—not a purse, but more like a knife in a boot. This dog represents the man's warrior persona. His world was probably full of violence and threat, and he has chosen a dog to both replicate that and offer protection from it.

A broken form of the Idealist would include those who drop pets off at the shelter when they redecorate their homes because the animal no longer "goes" with the furniture (yes, it *does* happen, and more often than you would believe).

Remember, a healthy and true Idealist would never even contemplate such a thing. No, she's more likely to slowly buy household accessories that complement her dog. In that way, her house becomes both a reflection of her passions and a salute to the dog she loves—comfortable and cozy, ordered and tidy. A good home for all who live under that roof.

You May Be an Idealist If You:

- Have trained the dog to stop inside the foyer to get her paws toweled off before proceeding into the house.

- Carry a collapsible water dish in the car.
- Feel just a little embarrassed by "doggie" behaviors even though you know they're natural: butt sniffing, trash eating, humping . . .
- Consistently appear in public without a single dog hair visible.
- *Always* have an extra poop bag for anyone who needs one, but you have to unzip twelve pockets—each with its own dog park necessity—in your Patagonia sport anorak before you can find one.

You're *Not* a True Idealist If You:

- Get a kick out of seeing your dog race through a mud puddle.
- Find wads of dog hair (and some loose change) in the crack of your car seat.
- Have ever been asked, "Do you have a yellow Lab?" based solely on the hair plastered to your fleece jacket.
- Have no visceral response to your dog sniffing another dog's butt.
- Don't need a Xanax when you realize you've left your poop bags in the car.

You May Be Headed for Trouble If You:

- Selected a breed of dog because you saw one on TV.
- Have ever changed your dog's collar (or, God help us, his fur color) to better match your outfit.
- Have even considered putting your male dog on steroids to bulk him up or have made him carry weights (in a pack or around his neck) to build his muscle.

- Have ever purchased a collar with spikes sticking from it or feathers attached to it other than as a Halloween costume.
- Have your groomer on speed dial, but not your veterinarian.

Favorite Names

Skip, Maggie, Molly, Walter, and other good, solid human names. Maybe a figure from history or literature who has a lot of integrity—Atticus (Finch), or Rosa (Parks), or Portia from "The Merchant of Venice" ("The Quality of mercy is not strain'd . . ."). Whatever the Idealist picks, it will probably end up monogrammed onto a bed, so the shorter the better. Watch for names from fashion for the accessorizers: Prada, Calvin, or even Orvis for some.

Sweet Nothings

When he's praised, he'll hear how handsome, how well behaved, how well mannered, how polite he is. And, man, will that dog puff his chest out with pride.

Tips for Training

You're likely to be attracted to methods that employ both obvious praise and clear, calm correction. "All positive" won't make any sense to you; after all, shouldn't the dog know when he did wrong? In your hands, commands are likely delivered with calm clarity and warmth, so . . . have at it!

Character-Building Exercises

- Next time a plan goes awry, say, "Oh, well" and stay relaxed.

- Buy a dog toy that has no redeeming value beyond the fact that your dog likes it—better yet, pick it in a garish color that matches nothing in your house.
- Try a new dog park, take a new walking route . . .

Breeds to Which Idealists Are Drawn

Popular and/or tidy dogs. Golden Retrievers are always high on an Idealist's list, as are Labrador Retrievers, Vizslas, Pugs, and Beagles. They just love a rugged, clean-cut, no-nonsense dog. Nowadays, the invasion of the Doodles has made them the Golden Children of this group. Unadulterated Standard Poodles, the ones who love to please, and who follow commands with such crisp flair, fit perfectly. These breeds will do well in the volunteer therapy work you are interested in.

Breeds Idealists Should Avoid

To an Idealist, barky, spinning, high-energy dogs just don't seem sensible. One possible exception is the Jack Russell Terrier, but Idealists should use caution—just because you saw one at your favorite horse show doesn't mean this dog will thrive in your house. Also, the breed should be true to the Idealist's perfectionist nature—a dog from any drooling breed that flaps spit in your cereal bowl or sends it oozing off your chandelier with one shake of a mighty head is not going to amuse.

The Idealist in Love

SOUL MATE—There have to be a lot of other things in common to pull this one off. It's not a matter of conflict and bickering; it's just that a Soul Mate may be a tad incomprehensible to an Idealist.

A recent study in Italy has revealed a funny barometer of dog emotion. In their paper, "Asymmetric tail-wagging responses by dogs to different emotive stimuli" (*Current Biology*, March 20, 2007), a neuroscientist and two veterinarians explain that when dogs feel good about someone or something, they wag more toward the right side of their bodies, and when they have more negative feelings, the wagging leans left.

Brain research in mammals (including us) has shown that our left brains seem to control happier emotions than the right. And because the left brain controls the right side of the body and the right side controls the left, the tail wagging makes sense.

This divvying up of positive and negative actions in the brain was explained in a *New York Times* article: "Thus many birds seek food with their right eye (left brain/nourishment) and watch for predators with their left eye (right brain/danger). In humans, the muscles on the right side of the face tend to reflect happiness (left brain) whereas muscles on the left side of the face reflect unhappiness (right brain)."

Presumably, when we greet our dogs, the right side of our faces and the right side of their fannies go into high gear.

EXPERT—More than one Expert has a dash of Idealist mixed in, so they'll "get" each other. Bowing to the Expert's superior knowledge (if they in fact have it) might stick in an Idealist's craw, though.

DYNAMO—This can work. The Dynamo will get everything done on both their lists, which takes some pressure off the Idealist's shoulders. With this Dynamic Duo, the dog, the house, the wardrobe—everything—will be kept to their mutually high standards.

ANGEL—An unlikely matchup. The Idealist just can't figure out how she could maintain her sanity with eight dogs in the house, one of them with irritable bowel syndrome and another with chronic anal sac impaction.

IDEALIST—An Idealist squared? Can we come to your house for dinner? A lovely home, a perfect meal, and delightful dinner conversation. We're there! What this pair may lack in raw chemistry they more than make up for in comfort and ease. Won't be a particularly challenging pairing, but not everyone wants that. Enjoy!

MASTER—Another pair that can overlap. Masters are pretty sober about getting things right also. The problem is the union could be a little too serious.

FREE SPIRIT—With enough physical attraction, these two might just feel some heat from the friction of two opposing lifestyles. They can be that cute couple who roll their eyes— playfully, flirtatiously—when recounting the latest antics of the other.

OBSERVER—Sure . . . why not? The Observer will watch a partner doing his thing and ponder it. That looks like appreciation for the kind of consideration the Idealist puts into everything. It probably isn't, but if the Idealist reads it that way, fabulous.

BUDDY—Whoops. Can the student government president find romance with the class cutup? Probably not. Sometimes opposites attract, but this is more likely a case of lost in translation.

#5 QUIZ: I TRAIN MY DOG BECAUSE...

a) I want to deepen our connection.

b) I want to keep her safe in this crazy world.

c) It's fun to watch him learn.

d) All life is training, so you might as well do it right.

e) I don't, I would not want to break his beautiful spirit.

f) My favorite instructor just started a new Basic Rally Class.

g) My vet said to, and I can fit ten minutes in between Pilates and picking Brittany up at soccer. Besides, if she's trained, things will go faster and more smoothly.

h) It's the right thing to do.

i) I'm hoping to get him to stay by my gear when I boulder on the weekends.

a) Soul Mate, b) Angel, c) Observer, d) Master, e) Free Spirit, f) Expert, g) Dynamo, h) Idealist, i) Buddy

The Master

Motto: Follow my lead!

Masters attach through working with their dog(s). At their finest, these Do-ers want to bring out the very best in their charges. They see their job as one of coaching, teaching, and leading. Patient and persistent, they can have well-behaved, well-adjusted dogs who are often the stars of the block—the German Shepherd dogs who will stop on a dime when called, the Standard Poodle who enthusiastically has mastered 200 commands.

For them, the rest of life is what happens in between training sessions, and few things compete with teaching for pure enjoyment. Other tasks, exercise, and play are done because they help the dog be mentally and physically fit, but they aren't as much "fun" for the Master as training. In fact, Masters often mix a little training in other activities, just to "spice" them up a bit. Here's a no-nonsense Master's commentary:

Sure. I have a dog because the relationship adds to my life. If she infringed on my life, I wouldn't have her. The responsibility she demands is something I need. I like to spend time at home; she is part of the reason. I enjoy teaching dogs and the way they learn. I started off in the obedience world, then progressed to agility and flyball (more because they enjoyed it, so it was more fun to teach). I own retrievers and their purpose is retrieving. Therefore, I guess I was drawn toward working certificates, hunt tests, and field trials. It is a joy to teach something the dog was bred to do even though I do not hunt (or have the desire to do it).

Straightforward and succinct, this Master (with a touch of Observer, it seems) clearly finds his connection to his dogs through their work together. You'd hardly call him bubbling over with emotion, but his commitment and enjoyment are clear. Our bet is he does an excellent job with his dogs, though we doubt they drink from bowls with their names on them or lounge on matching dog beds. And we also doubt they care about such things in the least.

In Dogology, the term *Master* is used in the sense of mastering or becoming expert at something, and also in having a need and the ability to lead. The best of these Masters are a joy to watch—the communication with their dogs is an open line. The dog never disconnects. That is, when the dog of a Master gets too rough in play with another dog, or is chasing a squirrel too close to the street, the Master just has to say the word to break it off. The dog is never "too focused to listen." You'll see plenty of Masters at competitive events, but there are also many "quiet" Masters out there. If they do regularly go to a public park, theirs are the best-trained dogs—and the wild thing is that even the other dogs at the park seem to behave better when interacting with a Master. That's because he signals leadership with his posture and every gesture. Really great Masters have charisma, and the quiet kind is the best.

Master in Dogology does *not* connote a Master/Slave connection (but for that, read on). At the center of any Master's mind-set is control—in a perfect world, control of self first, control of the dog second. Dealing with control is a necessary part of dog care and training, but it can be the siren call to a weakness in some Masters. Control can move to controlling, and then the slide down the slippery slope into the quagmire we call Warden begins.

For a Warden, training is not something you do *with* your dog but *to* your dog. It is ritualized combat, and the dog is the opposition. The dog is punished hard for any "infraction"—which the human always perceives as the dog's "fault." Since the goal for Wardens is absolute obedience at all times, they believe that their ends justify their means. Blaming the dog for any error in performance, they punish with confidence and press the zap function of an electronic collar with abandon. If they read this (though it's doubtful they will), they will snort derisively at such wimpy attitudes and smugly think about how much better "trained" their dogs are. Their dogs are a reflection—and victim—of the Warden's need to be 110 percent in control all the time and to work with beings who cannot protest or question their methods.

Sadly, there is a level of hell below Warden, and here you will find the human who blames others for his rage. Someone does something "wrong," and this person erupts. He may well have been the target of such rage in the past, and now he makes darn sure that he will never be in that position again. The trouble is—he's been infected. He perpetuates the very pattern he loathes. His partner, neighbors, kids, and dog are now in the crosshairs. But he holds himself blameless because, in his mind, they all did something that "made" him react.

Wardens seem more common in myth than in reality. Most Masters are striving for a better understanding of and communication with their canine companions, and no matter how they personally pursue that task, their goal is always what is best for their dogs. Hang out with a Master when you can; you'll definitely learn something. And Masters show all of us that training certainly does not "break a dog's spirit"—it does just the opposite.

You May Be a Master If You:

- Rarely go to the dog park (pet people can be so annoying) or, if there, are seen off to one side tossing a ball or practicing obedience.
- Say things to your dog once and then calmly make it happen.
- Respond to your dog's demands for attention by quietly redirecting the dog.
- Can eat without your dog begging in any way.
- Can be protective and fearless—for better or worse, you put yourself in physical danger to protect your dog from harm.
- Have been considered "cold" by other types.

You're *Not* a True Master If You:

- Say "sit" and your dog lies down and you shrug: Close enough.
- Are a member of the Macchiato Mod Squad (see page 210).
- Laugh when your puppy trots into the kitchen with your underwear in tow.
- Lie on the floor to rest your head on your dog (dog size permitting).
- Have ever bought a toy based solely on its cuteness factor.
- Have a piece of training equipment, canine outerwear, or collar that is pink.

You May Be Headed for Trouble If:

- You've yanked your dog off her feet, hung her, or hit her, and you think "she had it coming."
- Your dog is "in trouble" for being sick in the house.

- You scoff at pet owners as "ignorant" and "soft."
- You have put two or more electronic collars on your dog at the same time.
- You think your dog tries to "get away" with things or tries to "get you."

Favorite Names

Names from ancient mythology—Athena, Zeus, Thor—or war heroes like MacArthur or Churchill. If the Master is into a fast-paced sport such as agility or Flyball, the name will represent the activity (like Polo) or the hope: Bullet, Zip, Lightning.

Sweet Nothings

When he's praised, the Master's dog will be called the best, the most excellent, the smartest, or anything else with a superlative attached. The Modern Master praises abundantly—enjoying the joy he sees in his dog. If he's a traditional Master or sliding toward Warden, he'll praise briefly and roughly when he praises at all. After all, the dog "knows" what he did right.

Tips for Training

You don't need (or want) tips, do you? You already have your opinion and your method and so are all set. Our biggest suggestion is to get your hands on as many different sorts of dogs as you can (by which we mean both breed and temperament). Working with a wide variety and a great number of dogs is the best thing for honing skills and broadening your approach.

Character-Building Exercises

- Do something with your dog "just for fun" and then, just have fun.
- Go watch other trainers work and just pay attention to the things they do well.
- Force yourself to read *Marley and Me* all the way through.

Breeds to Which Masters Are Drawn

Can be any breed but not infrequently dogs who are a lot of dog: Rottweiler, Cane Corso, Chesapeake Bay Retriever, and the like. If the Master is into agility, Border Collies and "Border Jacks" (Border Collie/Jack Russell crosses) suit. If the Master is into obedience, high-activity Golden Retrievers will grab his attention. Masters pick more by temperament and "drives" than by looks. Belgian Sheepdogs and Standard Poodles are great matches, too.

Breeds Masters Should Avoid

Breeds or individual dogs who shut down easily—whippets, Scottish Deerhounds, Ibizan hounds, greyhounds—can frustrate, unless you're the type who enjoys a challenge and sees training as something you do *with* a dog, not *to* a dog. If you are that sort of Master, you may well love these exact dogs.

The Master in Love

SOUL MATE—Danger: potentially flammable combination. The Master will be accused of being too tough and the Soul Mate of being too soft, and both may well be more than a bit right. If each can appreciate the best in the other, things could heat up, but if not, there will be more doors slamming (the Soul Mate into the bedroom to cuddle with the dog and the Master out the door to run the dog) than sparks flying.

EXPERT—Hmmm . . . here are two dogs with their tails straight up and vibrating. If they connect in some way, a more formidable combo is hard to imagine. The Expert keeps up with every new method on the horizon, and the Master develops smooth handling techniques and puts in the practice time. But more often than not, it ends as most "tails up" meetings do: in a quick, noisy dustup before each goes his own way—stiff legged and hackles still up.

DYNAMO—Could be, if their lists overlap and if the Dynamo's substantial energy can be focused on training issues as well as life issues, then these two may be seen unloading PVC agility jumps at the local park, pulling up to trials in their well-organized minivan, or power walking their dog(s) every morning before work.

ANGEL—There's a high probability of a culture clash here, but if the Angel considers good behavior part of the "saving" process and the Master enjoys educating needy dogs—then that's a love match. Okay, that's a stretch, but we're trying to be positive here.

IDEALIST—Well, here are two who like to get things right. They *can* do just that together, but it'll probably be more of a play-by-the-rules pairing than a fiery one. Nothing wrong with that—you'll have a well-run home, well-trained dog(s), and a damn fine credit rating to boot.

MASTER—Two Masters can make it work, but it isn't common that they do. In order to find their way, they both have to be willing to work on the control of their own weaknesses and flaws more than the control of others. (And in some matters these two will just have to

All types have a soft side; Masters are no exception. ➤

agree to disagree.) If they find a way, they can enjoy shared interests and passions, so it's well worth the trouble. And it will be trouble.

FREE SPIRIT—Noooo, not a chance here unless both really feel passionately about wanting to remake their partners in their own image. The duo will last as long as the partner's tolerance for this does.

OBSERVER—If the Observer likes to watch the Master teach (and most Masters secretly or otherwise like to be watched), this can fill the bill for both. They can expect intense dinner table conversation about training methods and philosophies.

BUDDY—Hmmm . . . Master may enjoy the Buddy, but the Buddy is going to find the Master to be a drag. There's just no romance there. Master and Buddy would have a hard time taking a stroll together, never mind sex or marriage. And in the bedroom? More exasperation than perspiration. They may mesh as Mutt and Jeff best friends.

#6 QUIZ: YOUR DOG DROPS A BALL AT YOUR FEET. YOU THINK:

a) Where did he get that ball? Did he lose his Planet Dog Orbee again?!

b) He's grateful that I saved him. Aren't dogs amazing?

c) He knows I am sad and is trying to cheer me up.

d) What would happen if I throw two balls?

e) He's offering his toy to me because I am his leader.

f) He's giving me the ball; he loves to share.

g) Balls like that can get stuck in a dog's throat . . .

h) See? He wants to play some more!

i) Ball? What ball? [Doesn't notice the ball.]

a) Idealist, b) Angel, c) Soul Mate, d) Observer, e) Master, f) Free Spirit, g) Expert, h) Buddy, i) Dynamo

The Free Spirit

Motto: Let it be!

The Free Spirit attaches by allowing her dog to pretty much do what he wants. This Feeler has dealt with stress either present or past, and is into getting rid of it. Those with present-tense stress would include high-power successful people who spend their days making decisions. Nearly every person they come in contact with wants something from them. There is little "downtime," and there are very few "safe" relationships.

Enter the dog.

The dog is a haven from all of that, and as such, this type of Free Spirit has no interest in controlling the animal. The funny thing is that on the job she would never be called a Free Spirit. She makes decisions everywhere else, but not where her dog is concerned. So people who hold seats on the Stock Exchange, grace television and movie screens, and run the rest of their lives brilliantly can have dogs joyfully running amok. The best fit for this situation are happy, carefree dogs who can handle this much freedom without any serious consequences. This kind of Free Spirit will find many of the qualities of the other eight personality types in her character.

The second kind of Free Spirit we observe is working off past stress—where the dog gets the happy childhood the Free Spirit didn't have. This mythical childhood is one of complete freedom and acceptance, without fear, where love is unconditional and all behavior is "natural" and "beautiful." Some dogs can handle this, others—not so much. Here are the words of one Free Spirit:

Truly one of my favorite things to do in life is to walk into my living room, see her stretched out on her back on the couch, and have her not move a muscle as I sit down beside her and scratch her tummy. Then she'll stretch, give a low rumble, lick my fingers, and sigh as her leg starts going with the rhythm of the scratching. I love seeing her feel so safe and happy and healthy. . . . She is a great, galumphing, exuberant, goofy gal, and I'm glad she's spending this life with me!

Typical of the type, this Free Spirit loves the close physical contact and adores her dog completely, which is a pleasure to read. But what else is here? How about the desire not to disturb the dog? Does the dog have a busy schedule? All booked up, is she? The owner's concerns? Safety and happiness are first, because her lens has strong filters for danger and sadness. If her dog is "safe" and "happy," then all is well. Other types with different history might see things through another lens. An adult child of a messy divorce might list "feels secure," someone from a depressed home might cite "playful" . . . we're all a product of our pasts, and what we didn't have as children ourselves, we want to give to our children. For this sort of Free Spirit, that is freedom from fear, rules, and limits.

The writer above mentions a "low rumble," which will be heard by the Free Spirit as "talking" and could, in fact, be a benign moan/sigh of pleasure. But "rumble" is a tricky term to assess without hearing the actual noise directly. It could also be the rumble of a dog "scolding" the human for daring to intrude on "her" couch. Or it could be a growl in response to touching a vulnerable spot (the belly), which happily, in this case, the dog tolerates. Our concern is that the Free Spirit will never hear that as a warning because that is outside of his or her picture of the situation. If the dog is stable, things may never go beyond this. If the dog is not, the owner may be snapped at one day "completely out of the blue." It is a pattern that every dog trainer is familiar with—months of warnings that go unheeded and a devastated Free Spirit who just "doesn't understand why this happened; it's never happened before, and I love her sooooo much."

For those of us who have seen certain dogs enter people's lives just at the right moment to facilitate growth, the dog is actually offering this person a chance to heal—to find healthy limits and balance. Free Spirits do not like to be pressured themselves, so they hate to do it to others. They need to learn that a little bit of positive direction is part of love.

A healthy, balanced Free Spirit is fun and nonjudgmental. Although loath to set any kind of boundaries, he does lay down a few for the good of the dog. Patience is one of the most important qualities in a dog owner, and Free Spirits have it in spades. Despite the hectic world we live in, it is the Free Spirits who are the most likely among us to take the time to kick back and enjoy life. To a Free Spirit, getting lost just enhances an adventure. These are very attractive qualities to a dog. What a Free Spirit gets from a dog is the physical closeness he or she craves, and the chance to feel secure and not prey to judgment. The Free Spirit who is a little intimidated to express opinions freely, to rock the boat, or the Free Spirit who has to makes decisions and judgments all day has a companion who accepts all of his or her decisions. With a dog, the Free Spirit has to be the one to make a decision. He can't just say, as he might with other people, "Whatever you think, I think."

Or can he? This brings us to the Free Spirit's slippery slope—the Benign Neglector. The Benign Neglectors (BN) are an emotionally indulgent lot. Indecisive and afraid to take charge, they leave the parenting up to their children, their dog-owning up to the dog. Neither has the maturity or skill-set to take over. This leads to chaos and even danger. Instead of raising free spirits, they rear undisciplined brats (human and/or canine) who have no real concern for others.

BNs are shocked when friends refuse to come to their homes, family disinvites them if "that dog" is coming, and neighbors have formed a united front for leashes and against piles of poop on their property. A typical tale from a guest visiting a BN's home is how the dog leaped up into her suitcase and started digging through her stuff as the BN laughed about how "smart" her dog was and how he'd make a great airport security dog.

You know that ~~idiot~~ person who drops their dog off at the dog park and leaves to pick up the kids or do errands or whatever it is she does? That's always a BN.

While a Free Spirit would never dream of assaulting or harassing another person, a BN has no issue with her dog doing both frequently, as that is "natural" and the dog is "happy." She may feign regret that your white blouse has muddy paw prints up to the collar, but if she were really sorry, she'd do something to prevent it next time. But she cannot act. Indecision and apathy rule. That's the nasty Catch-22 of the BN: "Love" equals complete freedom, but complete freedom can cause problems, and if the rigorous application of more freedom doesn't solve those problems, she's immobilized.

Slide all the way down the slippery slope and reach the wallow where benign neglecting morphs into a form of New Age abuse. No longer simply owners who raise their dogs with so much "love" that the animals are unbearable as they leap, hump, wet, and slobber their way through life. These are people who can't bear to trim their dog's nails lest they hurt the dog, can't stand to comb out a mat because the dog might cry—and they don't let anyone else do it, either. They feel absolutely secure that they are doing "the best thing" for the dog, and they have no doubts about the course (or lack of a course) of action. And that's the New Age part. There is nothing new about neglect, but the self-righteous cloak these folks pull around themselves is woven from New Age thread.

Once someone has tumbled that far down the slope, they have lost the "free" part of free spirit, replacing it with rigidity of belief. Most of our Free Spirits stay way up high. Because they lead campaigns against stress and tension, they'll help you get rid of some of yours, too. They are wonderful people to spend time with and great friends to play with—no matter the ages of those involved!

You May Be a Free Spirit If You:

- Cannot get your dog to come when called. And when he doesn't, you shrug and say, "I guess we're staying!" (The important point here is that the Free Spirit really doesn't mind staying.)
- Say, when your dog leaps up, mouthing and pawing at guests, "She *loves* people!"
- Are often seen being dragged headlong toward other dogs as you call out, "He's friendly, he's friendly . . ."
- Allow the dog to sit on your lap while you drive or to race between windows barking at every person he sees or both in rapid succession.

You're *Not* a True Free Spirit If You:

- Have tried a new piece of training equipment to "get more control."
- Use a crate in the car. (Wouldn't that block his view out the windows?)
- Own a dog bed; after all, why would your dog want to sleep on the floor?
- Have watched *The Dog Whisperer* more than once.
- Have heeled down the street with your dog happily prancing at your side.
- Have ever gotten your Poodle an even remotely poodle-y haircut.

You May Be Headed for Trouble If:

- Friends have refused to come to your home because of your dog's behavior.
- Your dog has ever been out of your sight in a public park and you weren't worried.
- An article of your friend's clothing has been ripped or ruined by your dog's "happy" greeting.
- You've ever been dragged down by your dog—and you're definitely a BN if after that, you thought, "Well, he couldn't help that, he's just a dog."
- You've come home more than three times to a house that in some way was made worse by your dog being left in it and taken no action to change that fact (beyond discussing it with your dog at some length and trying to put things he might destroy out of his reach).

Favorite Names

The Free Spirit leans toward natural words—Breeze, Daisy, Dawn, Fern, Misty, Fawn—or optimistic names like Hope.

Sweet Nothings

When he's praised, the Free Spirit's dog will be an imp, an elf, such a naughty little dog, such a bad little dog, a funny bunny.

Tips for Training

Training?! You don't want to break your dog's spirit! Training is for control freaks—that's no fun!

Do us a favor, go to YouTube and check out Canine Freestyle Dancing. Yeah, we know, some of the outfits are a little out there, but look at how much fun the dogs are having! (And your dog might get some training, but you didn't hear that here.)

Character-Building Exercises

- Put a fence up around your yard.
- Schedule daily training time and stick to it for one month.
- Practice "come."

Breeds to Which Free Spirits Are Drawn

It's the energetic, boisterous, inevitably muddy dogs these folks crave. Free Spirits are drawn to dogs who model what they want the dog to want: to have fun, be free, enjoy the world. Look for delighted Doodles, leaping Labs, careening Cockers, and all manner of mixed breeds to be happily straining at the end of the Free Spirit's lead (when she has one on her dog).

Breeds Free Spirits Should Avoid

Breeds and individuals within any breed who are prone to aggression. Free Spirits are just not equipped to deal with this issue effectively, nor do they get any pleasure from doing so. Send those dogs over to a Master's house.

The Free Spirit in Love

SOUL MATE—Maybe a celestial match, as long as the Free Spirit is not irresponsible.
EXPERT—These are the two at the dinner party who can't agree on a thing and then, behind closed doors, shagomania! The Expert grounds the Free Spirit, and the Free

Spirit introduces the Expert to the senses normally ignored. Together, they provide a dog with a home that's both sound and sizzling.

DYNAMO—If one or both people medicate, this might work. Otherwise, not a chance.

ANGEL—Possible. Neither one will mind having a blended family—her three dogs and four cats added to his one dog, two cats, and a parrot. . . . None of these animals will be remotely trained, but since that isn't their desire or expectation, all is well. Just don't go over to their house.

IDEALIST—You know what happens when you add vinegar to baking soda? (Or Mentos to a bottle of soda?) Then you get the general gist. Let's spare the details—there may be children reading this.

MASTER—Not unless this is a Principal/Naughty Girl dynamic with striped ties hanging from the bedposts and a rumpled plaid skirt in the corner. If a certain type of Master gets to control and that certain type of Free Spirit gets to be controlled in a loving (albeit kinky) way, this privately happy pairing may be the head-scratcher of the neighborhood.

FREE SPIRIT—Oh Lord! Find a good bookkeeper and a willing housekeeper, then have yourselves some fun! Supporting and/or tolerating each other's neuroses is a mainstay of any successful couple, and you do that extremely well. Since you're not nearly as covetous of the dog as either the Angel or the Soul Mate, there is room in your life to share with another person.

OBSERVER—Sure, why not, as long as the Observer doesn't get emotionally beat up for being what she or he is. The Observer is unlikely to criticize the Free Spirit; that's not in their nature. That isn't to say the Free Spirit won't criticize the Observer.

BUDDY—Absolutely. But these two together need to do the world a favor: microchip their dogs because they *will* be misplaced. Buddy will choose the breed—a big, athletic, running dog—and neither will make sure the gate is closed.

#7 QUIZ: BITING THE HAND THAT FEEDS HIM

You're playing with your dog. As he gets excited, he grabs your hand pretty hard, but you're not injured. You think:

a) He just didn't realize it was me. Silly goose, let's play!

b) I read that grabbing is play as long as it doesn't break skin; that's how dogs learn to inhibit their bites.

c) He never learned to play properly, poor thing. I need to play with him more so he can learn how to be his sweet, gentle self all the time.

d) I command: "Back. Down." That was a mistake I don't want him making again!

e) That's not how we play. That's the end of that!

f) Last time I play this game with him.

g) Wahoo! Let's wrestle!

h) I could see he was getting overly excited by the game. Next time I'm going to try stopping a little bit before this point.

i) He didn't mean it. See? He's upset that he hurt me.

a) Free Spirit, b) Expert, c) Angel, d) Master, e) Idealist, f) Dynamo, g) Buddy, h) Observer, i) Soul Mate

The Observer

Motto: Seeing is believing!

The Observer attaches through watching. A Thinker type, she truly enjoys a dog in the process of being a dog. If you've ever just sat quietly reveling in your dog sleeping or parked it on a park bench to enjoy the show, you may have more than a thin slice of Observer in you.

Observers come in two common variations—the temporary (they've gotten a dog for the first time and are just passing through this type) and the permanent or "real."

Let's start with the Temps, since that is where many serious "dog people" often begin. They are newbies, unsure (or even clueless) about the animals in their homes. As one woman recently said at the vet's office where she had brought her new pup, "Dogs have different personalities?" Or as an owner of an eight-year-old Dalmatian exclaimed to Sarah after a comment on how the dog's tail position gave us information, "You're saying that what they do *means* something?" It can all be a mystery at first, and since dogs don't come with instructions attached (though we dearly wish they did), this is where we all begin.

These Temps are people who may go on to be very involved in the dog world, but are starting from scratch with their first pup. We're sure many of you reading this fit into that cozy category, so congrats on your new addition! To the Temporary Observer, everything the pup does is full of wonder. They want to know why the pup circles or scratches before she lies

The Shiba is looking off into the distance and the human is laughing—looks very Observer to us! ➤

down, why she teethes, if that's an outy belly button (no, sir, that's his penis), and so on. There is an old saying in the dog world that every new pet person has the perfect dog, and then we spend the rest of our lives trying to find or breed one just as marvelous.

Any of us can (delightfully) reenter this mode when faced with a new dog activity or situation. And that's one of the great gifts of dogs—you can go from Expert or Master to Observer by simply starting a brand-new dog activity. Skill in agility doesn't make you great at herding, and a fabulous disc team doesn't necessarily have any better understanding of problem behavior. You can devote a chunk of your life to the study of dogs and still never remotely know "all" of it. The Temporary Observer is an intense learning mode—think of it as the incubator for future Experts and Masters.

And while some people are just passing through, the people who live here think like scientists. Jane Goodall is a lifelong Observer, spending hours enchanted by the details and interactions that make up the daily life of the chimpanzee. Decades later, she is still watching, still learning, and we are all the better for it.

If you lose track of time when you are involved in something you love, then you belong here, at least in part. When Sarah went to her first dog show and sat by the obedience ring, the next thing she heard was a tired voice on the PA system saying, *"Sarah Wilson, lost but not forgotten . . ."* Apparently, Sarah's mother had been paging her for more than an hour, but Sarah had not heard a word as she watched one team after another go through their paces. If you read this and think, "How is that possible?" then turn to the next type, as you don't fit here, but if you nod and go, "Oh, sure . . . I can see that happening," welcome!

An Observer's idea of fun is sitting with a hot cup of coffee and watching her dog try to extricate a toy from under the couch. Where a Soul Mate would catapult from her chair to get the toy lest the dog experience a moment of frustration, an Observer sits back with a smile of anticipation, waiting to see what this bright little being is going to come up with. Consequently, Observer pups can be excellent problem solvers and aren't prone to behavior issues rooted in emotional enmeshment such as separation anxiety. That's a difficulty that can be triggered when the dog and owner are constantly in contact, physical or verbal—think Soul Mate, Angel, or Free Spirit. Such a thing is just not an issue for a solid Observer.

Objective, aware, and curious, these people can make terrific owners and talented trainers. They don't ask their dogs to be their emotional sherpas—lifting and lugging all the owner's baggage. Dogs in Observer houses live a generally projectionist-free existence. As long as the Observer's curiosity extends into care and feeding, these dogs have good lives, as is clear here from this loving Observer's . . . um . . . observations:

> *Each one has such a different and fascinating presence that I could just sit and watch them all day as they interact with one another, my husband, and me. Since we have five dogs, it is a constant wonder and such a pleasure to be surrounded by them. I look at their little sleeping faces and my heart melts. And when they run and tumble around in the yard together, I think I have never seen anything so joyous and simply beautiful in my life. I think more than anything, they help me to take the time to see and feel. Just their presence requires that, but I like to take it a step further and just bask in their "being" and their wonderful in-the-moment way of seeing things. I also love touching them and knowing their bodies by heart.*

This little love poem shows that Observers have real hearts—not just clipboards—inside their chests. The Observer who wrote this finds that her dogs take her from her viewing

Solitary confinement for life—no crime, no hope of parole.

YOU HAD ME AT WOOF

In a national survey conducted by the American Animal Hospital Association, nearly three-quarters of the married respondents admitted to greeting "their pet first when they return home."

That may shock some people, but, frankly, we cannot believe that 25 percent of people don't. We think they're lying (or they have fish). Anyway, who can blame us dog people? When's the last time your significant other ran panting to the door wearing only a collar?

post into the physical world—"I also love touching them and knowing their bodies by heart," she says.

The slippery slope of Observers, however, is toward that clipboard—the tendency to be a Bystander. There are plenty of stories floating around of cases in which a crowd of people watches some horrible crime occur without anyone lifting a finger to intervene. This is called the bystander effect. In the ranks of the disconnected, these dog owners stand motionless as their dog attacks another. They do nothing as others rush in to break up the fight. They are also the ones who don't notice major changes in their dogs, such as pregnancy. Sarah's dog PJ was rescued from the classic "bystander" situation in which the owner said, "I don't know how old those pups are; I just saw them walking around the backyard one day." Excuse me? You didn't notice that your Jack Russell mix looked like a watermelon with feet? You didn't notice when she holed up somewhere for days on end? That her teats nearly dragged on the ground? Now *there's* a bystander!

There is one last stop on this downhill slide, the dark side of Observer, which is a life of extreme isolation. This poor soul's motto? *You are born alone and you die alone.* No surprise that he sets up his dog to be isolated as well. We're not talking about tying a dog out so it can potty while you watch the kids or crating him when you are at work—we mean banishment. The dog lives the gulag life—in the backyard, or the garage, or in the more modern version, a crate for 23 hours a day. If he barks or digs, then he is punished—because this extreme Bystander sees the dog's actions not as acts of boredom and desperation, but as insults directed at him—damn dog. Bad dog.

We would ask that the isolationist Bystander either changes his ways or re-homes the dog—let him be loved. Chances are, though, that this person will not, in fact cannot, because what if the dog goes someplace where he is cherished? That would be unbearable to the isolated person, making him even more alone and miserable. No, he'll keep the dog in back or down below in a basement or garage, to live out life in some twisted form of connection where the dog is forced to replicate this person's narrow world.

No one reading this book would fall into that category (such a person would never pick up this book!). Our Observers are able to view any other being as a feeling, sentient being. Appreciating and acknowledging differences is a healthy perspective that benefits any relationship and is deserving of admiration in all who have that skill.

You May Be an Observer If You:

- Want to know why "the dog" always sleeps on her red blankie and never on the green one . . .
- Are a photographer who often posts pictures you've taken at the dog park. (Since photography makes the do-er into the viewer, it's a perfect fit.)
- Have coffee-table books on wolves and dogs.
- Keep the dog bed where it can easily be seen from the favorite chair.
- In the process of trying to change a dog's behavior, have charts hanging on the fridge that are filled out daily.

You're *Not* a True Observer If You:

- Respond to your dog's requests instantly.
- Have more than one nonsensical pet name for your pet.
- See your dog trying to drag a large branch through a narrow gate and a) go to help immediately or b) walk away.
- Know your vet's phone number by heart.

You May Be Headed for Trouble If:

- Your dog is tied up in the backyard for more than an hour a day.
- Your household help gets a bigger greeting from your dog than you do.
- You watch your dog run off without a call or a comment, as if glued to a TV program.
- You do no hands-on care of the dog, either hiring it out to groomers or just not getting it done.
- Your dog repeatedly gets ear infections, which are always really nasty by the time you get to the veterinarian. Then even though these infections cause him great pain, you miss it the next time, too, until it's so bad he needs to be sedated to cope with the cleaning. Yeah, total Bystander.
- You have no interest in or time for training, but you'll have plenty of both when it comes to yelling at the dog. To paraphrase the horseman Pat Parelli: People don't have time to do it right, but they have time to do it wrong over and over again.

Favorite Names

The Temp-type Observers may pick the popular pet names because they are just seeing how everyone else does it. So we'll see a Max, a Lucy, a Bailey, or references to pop culture, such as Paris or Britney. Real Observers with a scientific leaning may pick great minds: Edison, Einstein, Galileo, Shakespeare, Milton, Lincoln. Bystanders will name the dog for the obvious: Spot, Patches, Brownie. And get this: The most disconnected among them won't even bother with a real name, choosing instead Dawg or Pup.

Sweet Nothings

When he's praised, the Temp-Observer's dog will hear he's a good dog, a fine dog, sooo cute, sooo sweet. He might be told that he's like a human friend—"You're my best friend" or a "good little buddy." The real Observers are more likely to comment on how interesting, intelligent, quick, and bright the dog is . . . as those are the attributes he values and, therefore, notices.

Tips for Training

The Temps should find a compassionate, patient teacher whose students look happy (both the dogs and the people). Method doesn't matter as much as nice relaxed grins on both faces and a good tail wag (from the dog). A good teacher of any stripe will get the beginner started on the right track, since many methods work if you actually use them.

For the real Observer, you'll love the hard-core clicker work: You get to break behaviors down into tiny pieces, make a list on a spreadsheet of each tiny step, and then graph your progress over each training session, probably converting the data into colorful charts—oooo, what fun!

◄ Observers, in fact all Thinker types, can greatly enjoy teaching complex tricks—and are quite good at it!

Character-Building Exercises

- Invite a new friend to go for a walk with your dogs.
- Take a canine massage class.
- Sit on the floor and actively play with your dog.

Breeds to Which Observers Are Drawn

The Temp looks for a dog the way a junior high school kid looks for romance—cuteness is everything. Only after a few "dates" does the middle schooler realize that she may not even like the cutest boy in the class. So it is with the Temps—they may fall in love with a Weimaraner in a Wegman calendar or a spotted dervish from *101 Dalmatians*. The shock comes when the houndy hurricanes start to need more exercise, more training, and just more. . . .

The real Observers may be attracted to the social breeds, probably because these dogs can do things they cannot—make friends quickly, connect with others consistently. Such dogs will also solicit interaction when it may not occur to the Observer to do so—not that they don't want to, they just don't think to. Or they will be enchanted by the charming problem-solvers with whom there is never a dull moment: Shiba Inu, Basenji, Toy Fox Terrier, Boston Terrier, Miniature Schnauzer.

Breeds Observers Should Avoid

All Observers should steer clear of any breed with high daily hands-on care requirements or with temperaments that need consistent, active direction. Think Afghan hound in full coat, some Rottweilers, Bouvier des Flanders, Shar Pei, and Australian Cattle Dog or any other breed that generally needs a leader, not a watcher.

The Observer in Love

SOUL MATE—Lots of room here for true love if the Observer enjoys seeing the Soul Mate bond with, care for, and hang out with the dog(s) and if the Observer isn't jealous of all that attention going elsewhere, he or she might find a lot to look at, and the Soul Mate may find a lot of nonjudgmental support.

EXPERT—Possible perfection. The Expert wants to educate the Observer on everything she doesn't know, and she wants to learn. As long as the Expert doesn't slip into a

THE GIFT OF PLAY

When we get to a certain age (and it's pretty early), we rarely engage in play with other people. We're not talking about working out or competing or doing things because we need to or should. We're talking about exuberant play—the kind you engage in for its own silly, purposeless sake. Our dogs, on the other hand, are always up for a game. Toss some leaves and a dog says, "Wahoo! Great idea! I'll bite at them, do it again, do it again." He never says, "Jeez, you throw like a girl" or "Nancy does it better" or "I don't have time" or "I can't! Someone will see me." Dogs allow us to lose ourselves completely in the childlike state of play, and in so doing, we can find ourselves again. If dogs did nothing else for us than be willing playmates, that would be enough.

condescending tone and the Observer doesn't find holes in his theories, it could be a mesmerizing bond.

DYNAMO—Possible. If the Observer notices all the hard work of the Dynamo, and if the Dynamo's hurricane-force productivity doesn't batter the sensitive sensibilities of the Observer. We know of one such pairing: When both members of the couple work at home on the same day, the Observer retreats to a far bedroom to work. Still, the Dynamo has been known to stride into the room wearing a headset and yelling away in some phone conversation like *Mad Money*'s Jim Cramer. (Need we point out: The Observer hates this!) The dog in this household could develop a split personality.

ANGEL—Not a natural match, but there are possibilities under the right circumstances. Could work if the Angel likes to be watched and isn't so illogical that she makes no sense to our Observer (or, if a newbie, the newbie just believes what the Angel says—eventually conflict may erupt, but you probably have a good couple of years ahead of you).

IDEALIST—Absolutely! These two can go together like peas and carrots (to quote Forrest Gump). They both like to think things through, neither is prey to impulse buys, and the dog will help both get in touch with their softer sides.

MASTER—Deliciously, this can work as a perpetual student-teacher affair. But also as is the case with the Expert, an Observer who knows a thing or two can resent being lectured to all the time, and the Master can't resist any "constructive criticism."

FREE SPIRIT—Possibly . . . but the Free Spirit is rather free floating in his or her analysis of the world. If that's okay by the Observer, everything's golden. The Free Spirit always wants to be the MOST loving, MOST intuitive, BEST dog owner ever (exclamation point, exclamation point, heart, heart). The Observer (and any other type partner) must

accept that the Free Spirit will never be quite as close to her as the dog is, but for some Observers, that's okay.

OBSERVER—No conflict here, as they can both enjoy this new passion in life. Learning and exploring together, they will amuse each other while raising some happy dogs. Their personal limitations can become their relational lacks—meaning neither one can know how to reach out to each other or connect on a deeper emotional level. But if they don't miss that in their lives, then they won't feel it as a loss.

BUDDY—The Observer is like Type O blood—a universal donor. Since the big O likes to watch what people and dogs do, and the Buddy likes to go go go, there's plenty to watch. If the Buddy enjoys the freedom you offer, then you could parallel play for decades together.

#8 QUIZ: DOG PARK

While at the dog park, you witness a scuffle over a toy between a black Lab and a newly adopted dog. It was quick and no dog was hurt. You think to yourself:

a) That poor rescue dog is still insecure, I hope he feels better soon.

b) Hmmm . . . that black Lab isn't usually a problem . . . I wonder why he is so touchy today. . . .

c) Yup, that black Lab has been looking tenser and tenser; figured that was just a matter of time.

d) We're going to stay away from both those dogs!

e) Nothing . . . you don't worry about it a second; dogs squabble, no one got hurt, what's the question?

f) Why do people bring toys to the park? Everyone knows dogs get more protective over toys, that's just looking for trouble!

g) I'm going to change my walk time to avoid those two dogs.

h) "Summer, come! Don't go over there, no, please come, come on, girl! . . . Sorry!"

i) Oh, I'm glad my dog doesn't behave that way!

a) Angel, b) Observer, c) Master, d) Soul Mate, e) Buddy, f) Expert, g) Dynamo, h) Free Spirit, i) Idealist

The Buddy

Motto: Life is short!

The Buddy attaches through shared activity and—oh!—this is a fun group! Got a lot of energy and a little free time? Hang out with the Do-er type, if you can keep up. Expect to burn off a good number of calories (not that a Buddy thinks about such things), and a hunk of those calories will be lost through laughter.

The Buddy comes in several forms. The first focuses on structured play and the other on outdoor adventure. Some Buddies do both. Structured play means dog sports of all sorts. You'll find Buddy teams splashing through water tests, racing through flyball, or working on their disc dog routines. The outdoor adventure types could be skijoring or dog sledding through the winter and hiking through the summer months. But regardless of the form this type takes, what they share and how they connect is the adult version of shared play.

With his dog, a good Buddy is easy, unself-conscious, and natural. He doesn't "train," and yet his dog is pretty darn well trained. What the dog may lack in understanding of specific commands, he more than makes up for in mirroring his person's moods and moves. How does this happen? Simple, the Buddy System is based on the fact that these people are natural leaders, which is not lost on dogs. A prototypical Buddy is not prone to self-doubt or even much

Enjoying the world together. ➤

self-assessment; he just does what he does and brings his dog along with him from the beginning. The dog picks up on this clarity and confidence loud and clear.

But don't mistake this for a well-behaved dog. "Well-behaved" is not something the average Buddy aspires to—quite the opposite, in fact—so he can relate to his dog bucking the system. It is likely that, with his energy, intelligence, and high need for physical activity, school wasn't the most fun he had in his life, leaving him disinterested in anything that remotely smacks of being his dog's principal or, as he might put it, controller.

As I heard one puzzled Master type comment about a Buddy and her dog, "It's like she has a bear in her house." This Buddy owner, allergic to confinement of any sort (as quite a few Buddies are), has a dog who gets into cabinets and entertains himself by tossing around cereal boxes and bags of flour before settling in for a round of "let's move the couch." This Buddy just shrugs it off with a smile: That's my dog!

This is usually a one human/one dog (or occasionally two dogs) pairing. Wherever Buddy goes, his dog is sure to follow. The Buddy sits under a tree to rehydrate (a cool way to say drink some water), and the Buddy's dog flops down next to him. The Buddy goes rock climbing, and his dog naps on his pack or explores the vicinity, but doesn't go far. It's enough to make an Idealist scold, a Warden twitch, and a Soul Mate worry. But not the Buddy: The battle cry for this type is Fun! Not the most introspective type, their comments tend to be short and to the point:

I love my dogs and they love me. Not only am I the treat dispenser, we go fun places and do fun things. We get a lot of mutual pleasure from our activities (hiking, agility, pet stores, walks).

Basic and straightforward words that say it all—she sees herself as more than "treat dispenser," listing activities they share together, with a clear focus on fun. Yup, we have a Buddy here.

Whether urban or rural, the Buddy will be found outside with the dog jogging by his side on an early morning run . . . sniffing along as the Buddy heads for some bouldering . . . cavorting toward the lake in the shadow of the kayak being carried above the Buddy's head. . . . This is, when done well, an exciting and wonderful life for a dog. He may not be perfectly groomed; he may have a lead made from climbing rope; he may or may not have all his shots; but if you could ask him about his life, the dog would have no complaints.

Note: Not every dog/human pair seen scootering through the woods are Buddy—other types can enjoy this as well. What defines the Buddy isn't the activities they engage in, but the nature of their relaxed, easygoing, devil-may-care bond.

The slippery slope for this rollicking relationship is the casualness of it—or, put another way, his general "what-me-worry?" approach to risk can extend to the dog. This leads to the Buddy shifting downward into a Bozo.

The fact that a Bozo leaves the dog in his jeep with the windows wide open as he goes in to pick up a few more PowerBars and a liter of water doesn't worry him. He doesn't want the dog to overheat (which is good), and he never wonders what could happen. The dog has always stayed in the jeep before (which is true). He never considers that another dog could come up or that his dog might head off in pursuit of a passing cat or squirrel. By the time the Bozo comes out, his dog could be hurt or gone.

Such comments would make a Bozo shake his head—"yeah," he would say, "and I could get hit by a bus tomorrow, but I probably won't. I don't live my life worrying about

Clearly Bozo owned and operated.

what 'could' happen." And with that, such people are relatively immune to input from others—especially older others whom they see as non-risk-takers on their way to the undertaker.

A level below this are the dogs riding loose in the backs of pickup trucks, jogging with their owners on a scorching day, or running off-lead along a busy roadway. Such extreme Bozos think physics doesn't apply to them and that their dogs' freedom is more important than basic, commonsense[1] safety precautions. The perfect exemplar of this live-in-the-moment group is the band of Mt. Hood climbers who took their dog up to an altitude of more than

YOU COMING?

Quiet communion is one of the great gifts of dog to human. This is a familiar tableau to anyone who hikes with his or her dog. The dog has scooted ahead, and as the human comes along at human speed, the dog circles back to check in. The pair take a moment, dog wagging and accepting a neck scratch, the human gazing off into the woods, very probably lost in thought and yet in connection at the same time. They may stand together like this for a few seconds or a few minutes before, with a removal of the human hand and probably a quick lick to the human cheek, they are off again, into their world and yet together—joyfully sharing a quiet connection.

---

1   Common sense can be defined as experience applied to life, and since all our experiences vary, so does the definition of "common sense." For our part, common sense is not risking your dog's life for a bit of "fun"—we feel the same way about children jumping off the roof into the pool. The rush doesn't warrant the risk.

8,000 feet in February of 2007. It was fortunate for them that they did, since Velvet is credited with saving their lives, but the dog had no business up there in the first place.

Buddies should never be defined by the small number of Bozos out there. Buddies are the antidote to some of today's overly intense, overly involved, over-the-top caretaking styles. Kick back, have some fun, try not to worry so much—many a happy, fit, completely nonneurotic dog tags along with a carefree Buddy.

You May Be a Buddy If You:

- Take your dog biking, camping, skateboarding, skydiving.
- Allow your dog on every piece of furniture without qualm or question.
- Used to ride a motorcycle before you got the dog.
- Would have to admit that every chair and table leg in your home has a tooth mark on it. There may be paw prints on the countertop.
- Are more than occasionally on crutches, but always have a great story.
- Feed your dog whatever's leftover in the fridge: cold pizza, pepperoni, raw hamburger.
- Respond to the notion of a crate by saying, "Why would anyone stick their best friend in a box?"
- Know your dog's percentage of body fat.

You're *Not* a True Buddy If You:

- Neuter your dog without any urging from others.
- Keep your furniture dog free.

- Vacuum more than once a month.
- Don't know what a "carabiner" is.
- Wash your mattress pad (what the hell is a mattress pad?!).

You May Be Headed for Trouble If:

- You've ever given your dog a beer.
- You let the dog ride with his head out the window, in an open vehicle, or in the back of your open truck.
- You think everyone else is just a worrywart.
- You've taught your dog dangerous tricks like snapping at your face when you make a raspberry at him. You think this is hysterical and can't see the risks in this "game."

Favorite Names

Tough, fun names: Buster, Tug, Spike. Names of favorite sports and sports figures: Bode Miller, Halfpipe, Bonk, McTwist. Ironic names—Spot or Snowflake for the all-black Lab mix, Tiny for your Dane-cross, and Tumbleweed for that ungroomed Airedale/Golden mutt whom the Buddy refuses to call a "Doodle" until a friend points out he's Air-Doodle and now the Buddy thinks that's pretty cool.

Sweet Nothings

When he's praised, the Buddy's dog will be told he's a pal, a compadre, irondog, rocketman (or other phrases that point out the dog's physique, speed, and excellent condition), musclehead, or big butt. The loving "insults" are a big part of the Buddy patter, and the true icon of this dialogue is John Thornton, the graceful, masculine, and loving friend of the dog Buck in *The Call of the Wild:* "He had a way of taking Buck's head roughly between his hands, and resting his own head upon Buck's, of shaking him back and forth, the while calling him ill names that to Buck were love names. Buck knew no greater joy than that rough embrace and the sound of murmured oaths, and at each jerk back and forth it seemed that his heart would be shaken out of his body so great was its ecstasy."

Tips for Training

Disc dogs, dog scootering, skijoring, and backpacking all may appeal to a Buddy's let's-have-fun instincts. Go slowly, get experienced counsel, learn the new game, then have a blast—the dog will, too, if he's anything like his Buddy (and he is).

Character-Building Exercises

- Buy a doggy seatbelt harness and use it for a month.
- Take a formal dog class someplace fun.
- Brush out your dog, trim his nails, and check him for lumps.

Breeds to Which Buddies Are Drawn

Most typically rescued mixed breeds but, if purebred, think Australian Shepherd, German Shorthaired Pointer, Alaskan Malamute, and any other rugged, low-grooming-requirement canine athlete. If small, it'll be a terrier.

Breeds Buddies Should Avoid

Bulldogs, Bull Mastiffs, Boxers (the shortened noses make them more susceptible to heat stress), any long-backed/dwarf breed such as Dachshunds, Basset Hounds, or Corgis, who will be put at risk by miles of running and constant scrambling up and down and over. Any breed or mix that requires regular grooming to stay mat free and comfortable.

The Buddy in Love

SOUL MATE—If the Soul Mate's idea of connection is being outside with her dog, then this can work. But if the dog starts really getting into adventures with the Buddy, and even greets him at the door first—uh-oh. PS: Any time your partner gets inexplicably snarky, think back to see if "her" dog curled up with you on the couch—that'll cost you.

EXPERT—If the Expert's expertise covers knot-tying and how much water you need to carry

FUNNIER CAT OWNERS? NOT SO MUCH

One study published in 2006 in the journal *Society and Animals* concluded that dog owners laugh more often than cat owners,[2] which makes sense when you consider the moving parts: a wagging tail on the one hand and retractable claws on the other.

[2]*Society and Animals*, vol. 3, no. 14, 2006.

when hiking at 30 percent humidity and 90-degree temperatures—it's true love. If the Expert plans to lecture boyfriend Buddy on the risks and ramifications of letting the dog ride with his head out the window, forget it. He likes to ride that way, for God's sake, and nothing bad has ever happened!

DYNAMO—Excellent. You're matched in energy levels, and the Dynamo will remember to pack lunch and bring a map, two things you generally say are for sissies, but which you actually appreciate.

ANGEL—Another one-night stand for the Buddy! Surprise, surprise. (Considering how many one-night stands the Buddy has, you know he's hound-dogging *many* categories.) For the long haul, the Buddy's urge to go hiking in wet weather with the Angel's dog may be met with concerns for the dog's welfare—such as, "Does she have a raincoat?" and "Will it be slippery?" When the Buddy reasons, "She's a Labrador! She's supposed to be out in wet weather!" he'll be met with a stunned silence quickly followed by a torrent of angry explanations of how wrong he is, how mean he's being, and . . . well . . . if you want sex regularly, this probably isn't the best pick.

IDEALIST—This is a beautiful pairing . . . for a one-night stand (if the Buddy is gorgeous enough and comes from the right family). Longer term? Problems! There's no way to maintain a house that is both REI- and Martha Stewart–approved.

MASTER—Authority figures have never been a favorite of a Buddy, so, no way. The Buddy thinks the Master just needs to get laid (he's probably right, but he's not volunteering—everyone has their limits).

FREE SPIRIT—Wahoo! Ding ding ding! Here's a match made in heaven—Buddies and Free Spirits love without limits. The only risk is the Free Spirit getting her omnisensitive

#9 QUIZ: BEST SEAT IN THE HOUSE

Your dog is relaxing in a sunny spot on your favorite chair. You walk in and . . .

a) You shoo him off, because you don't want paw prints on your furniture. And he knows better!

b) The dog instantly hops off.

c) You go sit on another chair—after all, he looks so comfortable!

d) You smile . . . it's great to finally see him so relaxed and happy!

e) You tell him "off"—you know he's supposed to be lower than you at all times.

f) You scoot him off as you go to sit down—he hops off, then hops up on the couch. Fine with you.

g) You tell him "off," then move the chair a bit so you can put his bed in the sun. After all, that's what he wants—a comfy spot in the sun.

h) You scoot him off, sit down, and invite him right back up. That way you can both be comfortable there together.

i) You smile to yourself. At least he's comfy, and you don't have time to sit down right now anyway.

a) Idealist, b) Master, c) Free Spirit, d) Angel, e) Expert, f) Buddy, g) Observer, h) Soul Mate, i) Dynamo

feelings hurt, which the Buddy will have limited interest in and not much understanding of. But if they figure that piece out, this pair is the Energizer Bunny of type pairs; they just keep going and going. . . .

OBSERVER—Yup, let's get a move on. We're burning daylight! Added relational bonus: The Observer brings a camera and takes action shots.

BUDDY—Buddy-on-Buddy action—too much fun for everyone. The house (apartment/room in your parents' basement) is pretty much a wreck, but neither of you cares. No one can keep up with either of you, but that's fine—you love to work up a sweat together.

My Protective Type

There's something that dogs provide for nearly every owner: a sense of safety—sometimes real, sometimes perceived, but always comforting.

And you don't need a Rottweiler to do the trick. Even a tiny Chihuahua can let you sleep better at night. For women in particular, dogs are the guardians who allow us to relax when we are otherwise alone. In our houses, on long drives in the car, or out for walks, we feel more secure (and are, in fact, safer) with a dog along as companion.

Many of us hear some awful story on the news about a murder victim and think, "If only she had had a dog with her!" Lots of people have reached the same conclusion. In fact, joggers are so much safer with a dog that there are organizations that actually pair dogs who need exercise with dogless women joggers who need some protecting as they trot along lonely stretches of road. We don't know of any woman who doesn't feel just a little more secure on long solo driving trips when there's a pooch in the backseat.

That sense of safety ends up penetrating deeper—beyond our physical well-being, and into the realm of our emotional/mental selves as well. Dogs don't just scare off muggers, murderers, and creeps—they also help bolster a different kind of security by banishing loneliness, feelings of isolation, and self-criticism.

We each make a different stew out of all those ingredients. Because how we translate all this—what we want and need in terms of refuge and security—can be quite different depending on personality type. Some of us rely heavily on the security guard aspect of dog owning, while others mainly seek the emotional refuge of dog companionship. Most of us are somewhere in the middle, so let's sort it out.

Seeking Physical Protection

The types most likely to want a big, serious protection dog would be Master, Know-It-All end of Expert, Image Maker end of Idealist, Warden end of Master, Free Spirit, Benign Neglector end of Free Spirit, and Projectionist end of Soul Mate. Out of this group, only the Master and Warden could actually handle a protection dog properly.

The types who would be satisfied by the kind of watchdog ability most normal dogs possess would include Idealist, Angel, Observer, Soul Mate, Dynamo, Expert, Multitasker end of Dynamo, and Bystander end of Observer.

Types who don't understand the need for protection: Buddy, Bozo end of Buddy.

Note to all types: If you want a "protection dog," then cultivate your inner Master, but we remind you that the likelihood of a "bad guy" jumping out of the bushes to harm you is much lower than the likelihood of a friend jumping out of the bushes to surprise you, so get a dog for your real life. If that life is full of children, friends, and gettogethers, you need a social dog who will sound the alarm, not an asocial dog who is alarming.

Seeking Inner Protection

There is another sort of "safety" that dogs provide, a sort many of us don't spend much time considering. It's not protection from the outer "bad guys," but from the inner ones—our fears and doubts—things that often, for us "dog people," other humans simply cannot help us with. We all have them—they just take a different form in the different personality types. Here, by type, are a few ways dogs can bring light into our own individual darkness.

Soul Mate

You crave a sense of kinship, belonging, community, and home. Having your dog press against your legs at night, put a loving head on your foot while you read, and brush against you on walks puts those good feelings within easy and consistent reach. A dog's presence constantly reassures you that all is right in your world. When you have a good, strong bond in your life, nothing can stop you from achieving what you want. Soul Mate: You already know how to relish every molecule of this relationship. Keep it up.

Expert

For you, information is the key to connection, and if you just know enough, are smart enough, you'll matter. You'll find that sense of community you crave. That's a lot of pressure. Like the Idealist, you are comforted by the fact that a dog doesn't care about all that—she won't ditch you for a "better" crowd. Your dog adores you as you are, smart or not. Expert: Love your dog—and for fun, even act "stupid" around her. What freedom: She thinks your SAT score was perfect (not that we're saying it wasn't).

Dogs ward off all sorts of dangers, some of the worst of which live inside each of us.

Dynamo

In your world, being who you are may not feel like quite enough, but constantly doing things does. You prove your worth by doing, but your dog likes you even when you are sitting down. That loving canine presence reminds you to slow down and calm down in a way humans simply cannot, offering safe harbor (if only briefly) from the constant call of your inner taskmaster. Dogs are so full of love and approval that sometimes it doesn't even feel like cheating when you hang out and chill with them. Dynamo: Listen to your dog—she's right. You can live in the moment once in a while, and even though it feels so good, that doesn't mean it's bad for you.

Angel

If you are an Angel who never felt safe in, wanted by, or accepted within your family, dogs offer all three, every day. Notice, *dogs,* plural. Some Angels have one dog, but you more often have several, because after all, you crave family. Interestingly, the makeup of the group—in number and gender—can sometimes mirror that of the actual nuclear family left behind. But this reconstituted family is waaaaay more harmonious. Angel: You know just what makes you happy—being surrounded by your lovely and loving pack. The great thing is—and just ask your dogs—the feeling is mutual.

Idealist

Because you strive for perfection, you are your own toughest judge. Could you have done it differently? What will other people think? It's exhausting. That thumping tail, those adoring eyes—a dog provides relief from that negative and sometimes relentless internal Greek chorus. Idealist: You deserve a wonderful dog because you deserve a little self-approbation.

Master

For Masters, control and safety are one and the same. Dogs do a couple of things to boost that dynamic. By keeping you safe, they help keep you in control. By helping you feel in control—your response to an upsetting day may be to work with your dog, which puts things back to rights internally—they keep you feeling safe. Master: This is one area in your life you can control, so go ahead and work with your dog. You know it's about love and he does, too.

Free Spirit

For many Free Spirits, the dog is a total oasis from stresses past or present. A complete antidote. How can you not love that kind of complete refuge? Free Spirit: Go ahead, kick back, and enjoy. A little belly rub never hurt anybody.

Observer

The pit of despair for an Observer? Boredom. Observers live in their own internal worlds, but dogs are the rare creatures who can cross the border and gain access. They are good company there, offering a consistent buffer against loneliness that can haunt you in those moments when you think about it. Observer: There's nothing anti-intellectual about having good friends, like your dog!

Buddy

If you're a true Buddy, fear isn't a big part of your makeup—it's a waste of time you can't get back. Sure, you like having your dog on the bed at night as you thumb through the recent issue of *Outside* magazine, but it's not about needing comfort. No, no. Really it's not. Yes, Buddy, keep telling yourself that. Buddy: Can you believe you're even reading this section? You're the updated version of "I'm OK, You're OK." Go throw a ball for that pup.

Part 2

What's Your Breed?

The Dogologist's Guide to True Love

You've got your Dogology type nailed down, so now let's have some fun with it. Let's add another layer of understanding, another angle, a different perspective. Let's talk about breeds.

When we view dog breeds through the lens of our type, we can figure out some really important things. In this first section, we tackle which dogs we are attracted to and why, and in the second, we figure out which breed we ourselves would be, and which breed's characteristics we seek in a significant other.

In other words, these next two sections will help you find a dog, a mate, and yourself.

Choosing a dog is about falling in love. And considering your dating history, you might like a little help. Unlike those clunky and misguided breed-matching systems that get bogged down in height and hair color, this guide looks at the real traits that make a breed a true love or a true disaster. While most breed-selection books and computer programs couldn't pair two Argyle socks, never mind a person and dog, Dogology gets down and dirty and gets it right. We know love means being two of a kind or polar opposites, and that some pairings are just plain poison.

Note: The popularity of mixed-breed dogs is growing. Whether you've got a mix from a shelter or a "designer mutt" from a breeder, you can still sort out your match. To learn what home is best for your mix, read all breeds involved and combine as seems appropriate to reach your custom cocktail of traits and needs.

DOGOLOGY THROUGH THE AGES

Archeologists can trace the bond between dogs and humans as far back as 14,000 years. At a dig in the upper Jordan Valley in Israel, for instance, archeologists excavating a 12,000-year-old stone-covered tomb made a significant find. The bones there told a story familiar to us dog lovers: The remains of an elderly person were curled into a fetal position, clutching a 4- to 5-month-old puppy. Scholars may debate its meaning—was it an ancient version of packing a box lunch or some spiritual practice?—but we dog owners recognize the message. We know that we only curl around that which we love and from which we take comfort. That truth hasn't changed and probably never will.

Throughout time, there has been evidence of deep connection: When a favorite dog died in ancient Egypt, owners sometimes shaved their heads and bodies in the same mourning ritual that honored departed human beings. In the Hindu legend of Yudhishthira, the hero is allowed into Heaven because he refuses to enter without his faithful dog. The ancient Greeks were not known as the most humane dog owners, yet even among them, someone erected a tombstone with an epitaph in the dog's voice reading in part: "Laugh not, I pray thee/Though it is a dog's grave, tears fell for me." And Alexander the Great was known to have led a funeral procession for a beloved dog.

Many of us who are familiar with Homer's "Odyssey" may remember the story of Argos, the old frail dog who waited 20 years for Odysseus to return from the Trojan War—and though his master was disguised as a beggar, Argos was the first to recognize him.

In AD 124, the Greek philosopher and historian Arrian spoke of a favored female greyhound:

> She stays with me if I happen to be indoors, comes alongside when I go out, follows me to the gymnasium . . . and on my way home she goes in front, often looking back to make sure that I have not taken some side-turning: then, finding all well, she brightens and goes on merrily ahead again . . . When we are at dinner she mouths one or other of us by the foot, as a hint that she should have her portion. She has more language than any other dog I ever knew and can always tell you what she wants.

He knew, more than 2,000 years ago, what it feels like to love a dog and to move through the day connected to another being. If we ran into Arrian at the dog park, we'd all know each other, we'd smile at his hound's antics, he would listen to our stories, and we would walk along together—dog lovers—familiar and at home.

Retrievers and Spaniels

Retrievers: Labradors, Goldens, Nova Scotia Duck Tolling, Flat-Coats, Curly-Coats, Chesapeake Bay, Standard Poodles (really), Labradoodles, Goldendoodles

Spaniels: American Cocker, English Cocker, English Springer, Welsh Springer, Boykin, Field, Sussex, Clumber, Cavalier King Charles, the Toy Spaniels (not the Tibetan Spaniel or the Brittany, which are not spaniels)

Two of a Kind

You're family-focused, fun-loving, easygoing, and social. You've got an active lifestyle, but probably call yourself "athletic" rather than an "athlete." Your door is always open—you often have groups of people over, and kids stream in and out all day. Wherever you live, you see it as a safe, welcoming community. You love the wagging tail and big grin these breeds can sport and can't imagine having any other kind of dog.

Opposites Attract

You're shy or you didn't have good social connections as a kid, so you feel drawn to dogs who have the happy-go-lucky attitude you wish you had. If you're a beginner in the dog world, if you don't know how much training you are willing to provide (but the answer is probably not much), if you don't want to deal with aggression issues, look here—you'll find love! Of course, look carefully, because the overwhelming popularity of many of these dogs—Goldens, Labs, Springers, Cockers—has allowed some nasty temperaments and instability to creep into these breeds.

Bad Match

These dogs are so popular because they're so versatile. They can fit many people's hopes— they can handle even the neediest among us without too much stress. There are few "bad matches" for this generally Type O group. One would be if you are a "fawning phobe": You can't stand dogs (or dates) leaning, hovering, licking, pawing, bouncing, greeting everyone like a long-lost friend with a dash of tennis ball obsession thrown in. If so, these are *not* the dogs for you.

EXCEPTIONS: CHESSIES AND NOVA

In this cluster, Chesapeake Bay Retrievers stand alone—which is just fine with them. These are not the "love-everyone dogs" that fill the rest of this category. The best home for this potential powerhouse is with someone discerning, hard to impress, and who asks people to earn his or her friendship. Hard-living, strong in body and will, a supremely loyal friend, this person is a sought-after presence for anyone in a jam.

A bad match? Anyone who really should have a nicely bred Golden, but decides on a Chessie (it's a retriever too, right?). "Fasten your seat belts. It's going to be a bumpy night." Of course, the woman who made that admonition famous—the infamously strong-willed Bette Davis—could have handled a Chessie with one leash tied behind her back.

The other standout in this group is the relatively new Nova Scotia Duck Tolling Retriever. For this dog, you have to have energy to burn, intensity, and a quick reaction time! If you are equally high drive, high intelligence, and willing to work, then by all means pair up and we'll lay odds on who gets tired first. All laid-back loafers should take their delusions of athleticism elsewhere.

Pointers and Setters

Pointers: Brittany, English, German Shorthaired, German Wirehaired, Vizsla, Weimaraner, Wirehaired Pointing Griffon

Setters: English, Irish, Gordon, Red and White (red and white cousin of the Irish)

Two of a Kind

You're passionate and determined. When you get onto a good idea, you'll pursue it with unflagging energy, no matter whom you leave behind. When you're done working, you like your luxuries—a nice soft blanket, a comfy chair, and a good nap (though you may feel a little guilty about taking one). You think big, live big, and play big. You're rugged, but in a hike-all-day way, not a camp-without-an-air-mattress way. I mean, let's not get crazy about this!

Opposites Attract

You admire world-class athletes, and although you know you'll never be one yourself, you sure like watching them. You may well be a serious sports fan with the funny hats and body paint to prove it. You adore the outdoors (how would you have a picnic or tailgate party otherwise?)

and would not miss your weekend strolls through the local landscape. Watching your dog inhale the world gives you great pleasure, and at the park you sometimes like to find a good bench and watch him do his thing.

Bad Match

If you're more sluggish than slugger, if your appreciation of sports and nature is satisfied by ESPN or *Dancing with the Stars*, if your idea of daily exercise is jogging to the bathroom in the morning, this is not your group. You may dream that one of these dogs will kick-start your inner triathlete, but do everyone (including yourself) a favor and get a small dog. If you won't exercise the members of this group, they'll find a way to exercise themselves, and that's not fair to the dog or to your decorator. Also, if you're a rough and tough kind of trainer, be fore-warned: The setters won't like you and you won't like them.

Scent Hounds

Including Beagles, Bassets, Petit Basset Griffon Vendeen, Harrier, Otterhound, Bloodhound, Redboned Coon, Blue Ticked Coon, English and American Foxhound

Two of a Kind

Determined and focused, when you are on task, you are hard to distract (friends say "intense," enemies "relentless"). When not in work-mode, you are funny—a master of slapstick, and pegged as the class clown. Oh, and you do love food—when a hostess asks if there's anything you don't eat, you can't think of a single thing. You may be prone to a few (or more) extra pounds, but, hey, life is a banquet.

Opposites Attract

Cautious, careful planners who yearn for passion and spontaneity in life can gasp with shocked admiration when their hounds suddenly make a U-turn, followed by a mad dash to follow an urgent, pungent trail in full cry. They don't mind being dragged down the street behind their hounds; in fact, they find it rather amusing (most of the time). This quiet soul finds both the headlong, no-holds-barred run into life exhilarating and the curl up on the couch afterward totally captivating.

Bad Match

If muddy paw prints on your floor, a nose rising toward the countertop as you prepare a meal, and baying in delight when you arrive home sound like bad things to you, then a hound is a bad choice for you. Such things are simply "who they are"—like humans, don't pick one because your plan is to completely remodel them into something else. Pick what you find easy to love and then love it. Oh, and if you're in a Warden stage where you expect a dog to do everything you say because you say so, skip scent hounds for now, maybe forever.

Insider's Glimpse

> *I love the sweet houndy expressions. I love the way they run full-out, with all the joy apparent in the stretch of their muscles. I love the white-tipped tail and the unbelievably soft ears. I love the sheer joy in their tail wags when someone wants to say hello. I love their eagerness to learn, and their frighteningly fast problem solving. I love their open, friendly natures and their "four square" bodies. I love the sniffing, sniffing, sniffing everything . . . most of the time.*

EXCEPTION: DACHSHUNDS

Though this may make some people squawk, let's be serious: Any dog who is bred (and designed) specifically to go into holes in the ground to fight with animals below is a terrier. So Dachshunds are in the wrong place when they are thrown in with Whippets and Bloodhounds. For this breed, see Terriers, please!

Sight Hounds

Including Greyhound, Ibizan, Pharoah, Whippet, Borzoi, Saluki, Scottish Deerhound, Irish Wolfhound, and, from the Toy Group, the Italian Greyhound

Two of a Kind

You have a lean elegance about you and, although physically fit, don't have to spend hours working out. You do what you love and you do it well, but try to force you to do meaningless (to you) repetitive tasks and you're gone—if not bodily, then surely mentally. Curling up on the soft couch with a comforter drawn up around you while napping, reading, or watching TV is the perfect afternoon—if you can lounge with loved ones, so much the better (they love you even with your odd little quirks and obsessions). You never went to frat parties in college. You are the master of the one-on-one: close friends, not big crowds, for you. You'd rather walk through the woods with a good pal than drink and shout. What you choose to do, you do very, very well. You like your life just so: your things, your schedule, your diet.

Opposites Attract

More than any other group of dogs, the opposites attracting phenomenon is present and accounted for here. Nonathletic (often nonlean) people who have dreams (or memories) of fitness and grace are often drawn to these rangy athletes. For some people, their dogs can become their best alter egos, and they can take great pride in walking, showing, and breeding them. For others, who may consider themselves vertically challenged, the larger of these breeds represent the (literal) height of beauty. Our poster child for this is our own petite, feisty Vicki Croke, who lives life as a terrier but worships her towering Irish Wolfhounds in devoted succession. (What she does share with her wolfhounds is a love of quiet, routine, and extra sleep in the morning.)

Bad Match

Loud, physical people who want a rough-and-tumble, ready-for-anything companion can find sight hounds too sensitive for their liking. A house full of tumbling kids, high-decibel music,

EXCEPTIONS: BASENJI AND RHODESIAN RIDGEBACK

A Basenji is an out-in-left-field kind of breed. Different from anything else, they are little yodeling bags of quirkiness. If you want one, you must be playful with an independent streak and so genuinely funny that you can continuously tell jokes at other people's expense and have them laugh hard anyway. Then you'll be on the same page as your dog. Observers find heart-mates here.

Rhodesian Ridgebacks aren't like other hounds. Maybe it's the pointer, Dane, and other blood coursing through their veins. If you're happy with a handsome Rhodesian, you're probably a bit more rugged and outdoorsy than the average sight-hounder and more likely to go and keep going rather than go and go back to camp for a curl-up.

changing schedules, and slippery tiled floors would be an Irish Wolfhound's vision of hound hell. If any of this describes your lifestyle, give a Borzoi a break and check out Sporting Dogs instead.

Insider's Glimpse

He is Ibizan hound number 4 (Phoenix is number 5), so one could say I am totally "into" Ibizans, and I am. First there is the fact of their incredible beauty: They are art that moves, they stand out in almost ANY crowd. They are bright. Physically, Ibizans are everything I am not. Lean and long and built for speed and they can EAT, a lot, and still stay svelte. Yes, yes it's true—I live vicariously through my dogs.

Terriers

Every breed with the word "Terrier" in the name, including the Yorkshire, Toy Manchester, Silk, Toy Fox, and Dachshunds as well as the Boston Terrier from the Nonsporting Group. Exceptions? The Miniature Schnauzer, who is one, and the Tibetan Terrier, who isn't.

Two of a Kind

You are fun-loving, funny, determined, focused, and more than a bit active. Some people, amused by your impish charm, may miss the ramrod spine you possess, but it won't take them long to find it. They just have to open their ears, really, because my Lordy you can talk—especially when you're bored, lonely, excited, happy, frustrated, or angry.

You are amazingly versatile: as comfortable instructing the cabbie in midtown Manhattan on the series of zigzagging lefts and rights he needs to take to shave 3.4 seconds off your ride as you are organizing a trail construction project among the guests you've invited to the country house for a "relaxing" weekend.

If you enjoy rough-and-tumble games, even when they lead occasionally to crutches and casts, you're a total terrier person. But if you like the bark more than the bite, be careful to

EXCEPTION: PIT BULLS

This beleaguered dog is always a lightning rod for controversy. We're not going to attempt to wade into that mess. We'll just note that of the many people who enjoy this dog, there are two groups we wish would pick very carefully or pick another dog entirely.

The first is any Angel or Free Spirit who believes that "love" makes all dogs the naturally gentle, sweet creatures God meant them to be. The problem here is that God didn't make a poorly bred Pit Bull, people did, and bad people at that. You can no more "love" the desire to fight out of some fighting-bred Pits than you can "love" the desire to retrieve out of a hunting-bred Lab or the drive to herd from a farm-bred Border Collie. This doesn't make any of these animals "bad"—it makes them exactly what we made them to be.

There are always "Ferdinand the Bull"-type pits and look-alike mixes in need of homes. If your heart is set on a Pit, seek out such a gentle soul for a companion.

The second group is made up of people who learned early and well that no one was going to take care of them in this life but themselves and a few close, often handpicked, friends. Distrust for authority runs deep, often with good reason, and for them, a well-muscled, intact male Pit out at the end of the lead says everything they need said . . . and they don't give a flying *&*& what you think.

If you truly love Pit Bulls, educate yourself so that you can bring out the best in your chosen companion, making him or her an ambassador for this all-American breed. They need all the help they can get!

pick relatively low-aggression terriers like West Highland Whites, Miniature Schnauzers, and Cairns.

Opposites Attract

You're laid back. And though assertion isn't your thing, you do admire it in others—so you love your dog's ability to stand up for himself. Or you may be someone who wishes she weren't so serious about life, and your terrier's playfulness and gusto make you smile.

These bold, fun-loving risk-takers are the dream selves for many people. The important thing is for you to leaven the admiration with just enough training (we know, we know, that's not your thing) or supervision to prevent them from getting themselves into too much trouble.

Bad Match

Imagine being trapped in a broken elevator with Robin Williams as he takes his last swallow of a triple-shot Starbucks espresso and you discover it will be hours before repair people arrive. That's what life with a terrier feels like to the kind of person who likes to stay in her PJs all weekend. Go ahead, order a pizza. But most bored, undertrained, and underexercised terriers leave spit marks four feet up the storm door as the delivery kid approaches. They bark at you as you eat a slice. Then they rip up the pizza box just before they dig the crusts out of the kitchen trash. Bear this in mind: "Terrier people" find this funny.

Insider's Glimpse

> *My Jack Russell came to me after I had seen several nice pups from one breeder go through training classes. I had been attracted to the breed for some time because of their jaunty, feisty attitude, quick mind, and high energy, so I gave that breeder a call on impulse one day . . . I took her home "on a trial basis"—ha ha ha—and she has been a treasured family member ever since.*

Personal and Property Guards

Including Great Dane, Mastiff, Bull Mastiff, Cane Corso, Presa Canario, Boxer, Akita, Doberman Pinscher, Standard and Giant Schnauzers, and the Lhasa Apso from Nonsporting (better believe it . . .)

Many of the herding breeds have the potential and inclination as well, such as the German Shepherd Dog and the Belgians (all makes and models). Add to this some of the versatile sporting breeds such as the Chesapeake Bay, the German Shorthaired and Wirehaired Pointer, the Weimaraner. And although they don't have the size to pull it off, they will die trying: the Miniature Pinschers.

Two of a Kind

There are many personality types that fit the bill—everyone from the soccer mom with four kids to the athletic college kid. But they all find a home in this category because they have one thing in common: There's at least a little part of them that is guarded about the dangers of the outside world. If this is you, you believe, as a friend of Sarah's used to, that you should "always look on the dark side—you'll never be disappointed." You prepare for the worst. Not that you don't have fun with your friends and family, just that you know what human beings are capable of and you are vigilant when it comes to protecting what is precious to you. You may hang out with your one or two friends in the group, but you don't play the host. Your inner doormat reads: *Get out and stay out!* and your real-life one may as well.

Opposites Attract

You wish you could tell people to stop dropping by or calling or intruding on your time, but it's just not in you. You swallow your stress about it, smile, and say, "Okay." You're polite at all costs, including if it costs you a bit of yourself. You can't tell who is sincere and who isn't, so you worry that you're being taken advantage of, and you often are. In your heart, you're a bit frightened of this dog, but it gives you a secret rush when he erupts at the door in powerful barks. Controlling him is even more of a rush—not that you control him too quickly: You rather like that look of fear that flashes on people's faces. You'll deny that you do, but you do.

SPOKESDOG

So, all those Image Makers are right: People do judge you by the breed of dog you walk. In a study reported in a 2004 paper in the journal *Anthrozoös* titled "Spontaneous trait transference from dogs to owners," by Lynda Mae, Leah E. McMorris, and Jennifer Hendry, researchers at the University of Southern Mississippi investigated whether we attribute perceptions of certain breeds to their owners, and how we do it.

Of course there isn't universal agreement on the personalities of many breeds, but eight stood out by getting very uniform reactions.

If you're looking to shape your public persona, you'll want to know the characteristics consistently attributed to these breeds (and, in guilt or honor by association, their owners):

Poodle: Spoiled

Doberman: Aggressive

Cocker Spaniel: Friendly

Bulldog: Lazy

Chihuahua: Nervous

Golden Retriever: Intelligent

Jack Russell Terrier: Hyper

Collie: Heroic

Bad Match

Anyone confused about leadership (clarity and assertiveness) needs to look elsewhere for a companion. If you can't step up to the plate, back away from taking in one of these dogs. Or, if you're someone who doesn't have control over your anger (or if you use training as an excuse to get angry), don't come here—you may find you've bitten off more than you can put a compression bandage on. You may be attracted to this group's looks and watchdog abilities, but you aren't ready yet. You want one? Go earn your stripes. Get an easier-to-manage dog—like a Sporting Breed—and see what you can do.

Insider's Glimpse

> *Basically, I found nearly every aspect of the Akita personality—independence, reserve, quiet, self-assurance—to be a positive, though I realized I'd have to work extra on training and socialization to keep what I saw as positives from becoming negatives. The guardian heritage was something I simply saw as something to accept and work around to get the rest of the package. . . .*

Nordic Sled Dogs

Including Siberian Huskies, Malamutes, Spitz, Samoyed

Two of a Kind

On Fridays after work—if you indeed hold a steady job—you're out the door, hiking boots in hand, headed off to your favorite place on Earth: outside. You're good-looking, in an unprimped way, and the attention the other sex pays you is flattering but hardly distracting. You've left others in the dirt your whole life, and you still fail to understand why they don't just keep up. You love a great team game, but if some poor soul plays dirty or breaks a rule, you'll have none of it. After the dust settles, though, things are quickly forgiven—wanna beer?

Opposites Attract

You like to be playful and spontaneous, at least in theory, but it just never seems to quite happen. You don't feel light on your feet or free in your own body, but, boy, do you love watching a Siberian Husky be both. Through her, you touch a little bit of the wild every day. You keep your dog carefully groomed and have several hair-removing items in your home (and actually use them). This dog's biggest gift? He makes you feel special because he has chosen you to be his friend.

Bad Match

If you're the human version of "press 'n seal" (i.e. clingy) looking for the love of your life (which is exactly what you're doing), then be prepared to be disappointed—again. To avoid having to hire a new therapist, look at those congenial retrievers or a devoted toy for all the meaningful eye contact you could ever dream of. If you're a controller who is at the "do it or else" end of that range, both you and the dog will want out of this pairing. If you are in that group but have managed to keep your sense of humor and mental flexibility, you may find these dogs a fun challenge.

Insider's Glimpse

> I love a dog with personality and their own sense of themselves, if that makes any sense. Huskies always seem to have that; they are independent, mischievous, and so smart—but they are also extremely trusting and loving. In a moment they go from the fluffy demon who decided to eat a hole in your couch to the loving couch potato who just wants to snuggle next to you on the bed. I love their activity level, and nothing gives me more pleasure than sitting and watching a husky play in the backyard. . . .

Flock Guards

Including Kuvasz, Komondor, Akbash, Anatolian Shepherd, Great Pyrenees, Tibetan Mastiff

Two of a Kind

You have a fence around your yard or dearly want one. You have a loaded gun close at hand or have a baseball bat under the bed. You've kept childhood friends and always will. You do make friends, but it takes a few years to let them in the circle. You are the embodiment of loyalty, and you "might" fit well into the military (as long as you have rank!). You rarely find reason (or desire) to leave home.

Opposites Attract

You don't quite feel safe in your own home—unless a huge dog like this is resting by the door. Their classic night barking may bother your neighbors, but for you it is comforting. The risk you run is one of being seen as a member of their flock to guard rather than a leader to follow, so be careful. Any dog, left to her own devices, reverts to her genetic heritage. With flock guards, that can mean some pretty scary stuff. So love them all you want—just make sure that love comes in the form of ongoing socialization and training.

Bad Match

Oh, you love these dogs because they are such big, cute mountains of white fluff. Your idea of training is having your dog sit for an organic, handmade dog cookie—which you'll give him even if he doesn't feel like sitting. Just look at that squishabelicious face and eyes like pools of melted chocolate! Anyway, who cares, all a dog needs is love, right? Bad, very bad match.

Draft/Rescue Dogs

Including Newfoundlands, Bernese Mountain Dogs,
Saint Bernards

Two of a Kind

Sturdy—that term applies to the physical self, mental capacity, and emotional resilience. Or in your case, all of the above! You were a late bloomer but are finishing strong. You keep others' needs foremost in your mind, and if someone requires your help, you're there—and you don't pause at the vanity mirror on the way out the door! You're a thoughtful person, not prone to quick decisions.

Opposites Attract

You're the kite and this dog is your anchor. Flighty fits you, if you were to stop long enough to contemplate such a term. You're intuitive, mercurial, and funny. People are always surprised that you have this dog, but you're not. When you rest your hand on that snoring head, you can finally slow down, calm down, and feel comforted.

Bad Match

Mean-spirited people. These dogs just won't understand, at all, and will be quite broken-hearted.

Toys

The Toy Group is determined more by size than by task. If you're small, you're generally a Toy. The task they all have now is companionship, but they started out in different arenas. The Yorkie is a Terrier, the Italian Greyhound a Sight Hound, the Pomeranian a Nordic, and so on. So, this is a hard group to sort out. If you've got a Toy, or want to get one, read this section plus the entry that covers your dog's particular ancestry.

Two of a Kind

You want to be pampered and loved. You want the world to think you're cute (and you know what? It does!). You have way more charm than body mass. You want a significant other to dote on you, call you "baby," and do all the heavy lifting financially and physically. Nothing is ever your fault—it could all be easily explained away . . . if you could just explain. But you rarely have to explain because of that incredible charm. Ignoring you is unthinkable rudeness—after all, you mean well and meaning well excuses everything, right?

Opposites Attract

You want to be Mommy or Daddy in this world, to take care of defenseless little things, dress them up, but never dress them down. You have an eagle eye for what is going on around you, run your world with great clarity and determination, and expect great loyalty in return. You want complete control, no questions asked, because you believe that if everyone just did it *your* way, the world would be a better place anyway, so stop whining!

Bad Match

You played with stuffed animals, not dolls, as a kid. You don't like to fuss over things, and at this point in life you don't want to watch where you're walking because you might squash a loved one under your heel. You want a dog to fetch a tennis ball, not get bowled over by one. You want an equal, not a dependent. Your comments about Toy dogs include: "That's not a dog, that's a rat," "Add some barbeque sauce and that might make a pretty good meal," and the old classic, "A 'real' dog takes a **** bigger than that."

Insider's Glimpse

> *I got Julian after my elderly Yorkie (who had been a shelter rescue) passed on. I'd never had a Yorkie pup and it was a bit of a shocker, but we made do. Now, even though he can be a stinker, I can't imagine not having that little bit of chaos around.*

Nonsporting

This is a catchall group of dogs that is not organized around a single purpose. Many gathered here could just as well be included under another heading. Standard Poodles, for example, are versatile Retriever types, plain and simple; Dalmatians are Property Guards. Instead of addressing the whole group, we'll take a spin through the most popular members.

Poodles

Two of a Kind

You did well in school (though with your quick mind, you were a little bored). You're an easy athlete, a graceful mover, a fabulous dancer. You're neat, you're organized, and you have a classic sense of style. In fact, there's so much you do well, you'd think envious people would hate you. But they don't—you're too nice!

Opposites Attract

You appreciate athleticism because you have to work at it yourself. You may tend toward overweight and thrill at the sight of your dog—light as a feather, nimble as a gymnast—

chasing a ball. And you may even be a little shy, but you're proud as can be of the easy confidence your prancing dog displays—"She's such a people person!" everyone says of her. One subgroup of people in this category is made up of manly men who have a strong enough sense of themselves to proudly sport a poodle, pink ribbons or no pink ribbons.

Bad Match

If you'd rather rest than move, if you never score well watching *Jeopardy*, if you're naturally clumsy, if you care what other people think about your dog's haircut—move along. Nothing to see here.

Insider's Glimpse

> *My favorite qualities about Poodles are how smart they are in a people sort of way. . . . It just seems like Daphne picks up on language quicker, and the way her thought process works seems more "human." . . . Also, their sense of humor—they love to have fun! Poodles are also very athletic, and most people don't see beyond the fluff to realize that.*

Bulldogs

Two of a Kind

You're not traditionally good-looking, perhaps, but you have your own style and flair. You plow through life, undaunted by the little obstacles in your path. You're generally a Bulldog in a china shop. You don't get overly excited about much, but when something has your attention, it has it fully. Your competitors—in business or sports—may find they have greatly underestimated your quickness, intelligence, and determination.

Opposites Attract

You're active, svelte, and a little too distractible. People may be attracted to your refined good looks, but it's substance that you crave in others. Your Bulldog is the little tractor who keeps you on course.

Bad Match

Anyone who likes to run in the heat. Anyone who can't appreciate a jaunty underbite. Anyone too genteel for the rollicking, snorting, snoring, and farting that this breed provides.

Dalmatians

Two of a Kind

You're a lean, mean running machine. When others fall to the wayside, you just keep on jogging along. You stick close to your friends and tend to see others as questionable until they prove themselves otherwise. You can have a good time, but generally with good pals rather than in a crowd of strangers.

Opposites Attract

You don't feel traditionally pretty or possibly athletic, but you adore this dog's stylish, unusual look. You own some version of *101 Dalmatians* and know all the pups' names by heart. You do not get tired of watching your Dal move, play, sleep, run. You probably have tried your hand at agility because you so enjoy being with your dog—and he's *so good* at it.

Bad Match

You think you'd look pretty cool tooling this flashy breed around town. Your attraction is purely physical, and like so many such attractions, it does not take the dog's needs into consideration. If this animal could just be the art deco piece you had in mind, it would be perfect, but it turns out it sheds (constantly and profusely), barks, digs, runs, jumps, and might just be a little snarky! No one told you this!

Chows

Two of a Kind

You're not athletic and your look may be a slightly acquired taste, but for those who have acquired it, there is no other. It is no surprise that Martha Stewart loves these dogs. Dignified and self-contained, this is a breed that loves you and only you. Their interest in passing strangers (that would include everybody but you) is passing and sometimes a little strange. Funny, you have that same take on most people: If someone has something to offer you, great—if not, keep moving. You don't give much warning before you lose your temper—a light freeze? a hard look?—but when you do fire, it's for real. No one will forget it.

Opposites Attract

No matter how you feel, you always have a smile on your face—but you'd like to change that. You don't want to be so damn accommodating anymore. You'd like to be able to show some of your dog's self-contained distant air, but you just can't quite pull it off. You also like that he isn't friendly to everyone—that makes you feel special and loved.

Bad Match

Your door is always open to anyone in the neighborhood? Stick with open-door dogs like Retrievers and Spaniels: They'll celebrate your "come one, come all" policy. Athletic folks who want a canine companion for their runs, hikes, and climbs should leave the poor Chows (even a shaved one) alone and find a dog built for such things.

Insider's Glimpse

Legend was a bit of an impulse acquisition. I saw him, and as anyone who has seen a Chow puppy can attest, they're adorable. I did have knowledge of the breed, though. And I've never once regretted getting him in all of our 11 years together (and hopefully many more to come). I don't think a dog has ever fit more perfectly into a home than he did. He's always been calm and able to go anywhere with me. He put up with training classes, even though he found them silly. And he's always happy to offer some hugs and just be near you.

Herding Dogs-Sheep

Including Border Collie, Collie, Australian Shepherd, German Shepherd Dog, Old English Sheepdog

Two of a Kind

You have a high IQ and a lot of drive, and you like to control what's going on around you—but only for everyone's own good, of course. You're known to get your way without anyone even knowing your way was being gotten. If that doesn't work, you'll flash a little tooth if necessary. You can switch gears and react fast—snakebite fast—and before the recipient realizes what hit him, you are off and on to other matters. You've been accused more than once of being intense. But you just don't get that: I mean, you're only trying to make things right. Right? Right? Others have called you neurotic, and you kind of agree with them there. If you watch a scary film, you'll have bad dreams about it for weeks. You are sensitive to your friends' feelings, can read an expression from 30 paces, and never miss a trick. Your gut instincts are usually right—heck, *you're* usually right, or at least you'll go to your grave thinking that. You love complicated word games like Scrabble, and you're not competitive at all . . . as long as you're winning.

Opposites Attract

You are calm, unflappable, unconcerned, and unworried. People might call you uncreative, maybe even unexciting, but never neurotic. You sleep in on Sundays and any other day you can get away with it—though your dog will get you up! You may not be quick in your movements, but the *New York Times* Sunday crossword puzzle doesn't stand a chance against your fast-moving pen.

Bad Match

If you don't want to be so "on" mentally all the time with your dog, run—don't walk—in the opposite direction. Living with these breeds is a little like rooming with the captain of both the debate and cross-country teams. The easily frustrated should take a pass as well, as these dogs are complex and will feed you humble pie with a fork.

Insider's Glimpse

> *I have this visceral attraction to the herding breeds. I can't easily identify what it is that I love about them. However, it is definitely centered on their work ethic, their connection to their people, their intelligence, and their athleticism. What I love about the dogs that I have is their calmness, their confidence, their focus, and their deep attraction to me. Both Rascal and Sheena have had, and continue to have, issues that need to be worked through. However, I don't think that it has ever occurred to me that they couldn't be worked through.*

Herding Dogs-Cattle

Including Australian Cattledog, Kelpie, Corgis (both), some Australian Shepherds, some Border Collies

Two of a Kind

You're tough as nails and no one could ever fail to see you coming! You walk with a swagger, and you happily trade in finesse for effectiveness. You have a sturdy build and sensible exterior—not flashy but solid. You can work all day. You're a great poker player, probably an ex-smoker (maybe not so ex), and you know more than a few creative curses. Not prone to being overly demonstrative in public, you'd give your life for a loved one without a second thought (or the ability to have a second thought). You're the absolute epitome of "still waters run deep."

Opposites Attract

You saw this dog in *Mad Max* next to a young Mel Gibson and wanted one (or the other). You're neither tough nor cool—but you'd like to be more of both. You might have been that kid at school who got picked on year after year for no apparent reason, and that stays with you. A bit of a drama queen now, you admire this dog's quiet calm and unquestioning loyalty.

Bad Match

You're the weak link, a weakling, and a waffler. You're not sure of yourself, you don't assert yourself, but you apologize if you think you've even come close. You are love-hungry and cannot turn down a dog who wants attention or to play. You're used to people disrespecting you, so you don't even notice when this dog does so with a body block or a quick clip when running by you—"He's just enthusiastic!" you say. No, he's not. You're not much of a chess player, and people who can see several moves ahead baffle you, so don't choose a dog who can play eight or more moves ahead.

Breeding Love and Contentment

You understand the breed or type of breed you are attracted to in a dog? Great! You are on your way to understanding yourself and the mates you are drawn toward. Usually, we seek our complement in those closest to us: dogs or spouses. Though sometimes we seek an emotional mirror image.

What we know is that if you make a list of the characteristics you love most in your dog, it will also apply to what you want in a significant other.

You love Labs? Look for a man who is sporty, straightforward, and even-tempered. Greyhounds get you? Check the local café for the poet in a beret. Terriers turn you on? Stop at nothing less than the party guy who does everything in the extreme.

Stroll through the Love and Contentment section, and you'll have the blueprint for a great relationship—how to select and care for a mate, and instructions for them on how you want to be treated.

Retrievers and Spaniels

Joy to the world

Your Significant Other Is Like a Retriever/Spaniel

She needs to go out into the world and be with people. She finds social situations energizing and . . . she's popular! Without a mean bone in her body, she's not one to gossip or hold forth. She remembers birthdays and anniversaries, so she's a great catch if you don't. With a few notable exceptions, she's not a fighter and may be crushed when you take a harsh tone with her. For her, it really does feel like that's the end of the world. Oh, and, by the way, she really is just a flirt. She doesn't mean to be; she just is and doesn't mean a thing by it.

You Are Like a Retriever/Spaniel

Be careful! Not everyone in the world is as kind and sincere as you are. You'll never be very good at office politics because you prefer to say what you think and you tend to think good thoughts. You're a hard worker, taking direction well, and you make a reliable and dedicated "second in command." Once in a job you like, you hate to think of leaving it. That's just not who you are—hey, want to throw a ball around, then kick back with a couple of beers?

Pointers and Setters

Don't fence me in

Your Significant Other Is Like a Pointer/Setter

If you love somebody, let them go. They like to run and they have big ranges. If you want a partner who loves you, but doesn't cling, this may be a good fit. Don't take it personally—a Pointer/Setter doesn't stay home with anyone, except to rest up. While there may be a casual jogger or two in these ranks, more often they are serious runners whose legs piston up and down like they are on a mission. They may seem to be just circling around, but once they find what they are looking for—bang!—they're on it and stay on it until the task is completed.

You Are Like a Pointer/Setter

Just understand that the rest of the world doesn't understand. What they may think of as taking time to "find yourself" is really time spent sorting out priorities, and when you do hit your stride, you are something to behold. Plenty smart about the things you are interested in, you tend to "posthole" knowledge—deep understanding of a few narrow areas. You love your home and your family, but can't spend every waking minute with them—you need to get out and go, on a regular basis. And a wise partner lets you go because, let's face it, you're a royal pain if you don't.

Scent Hounds

Auto focus

Your Significant Other Is Like a Scent Hound

When she sets her mind on something, you have a determined force to be reckoned with. She's bright and a good problem solver. Once you have her attention (and it's not always easy), there will be no stopping her—she'll get done what she thinks needs to be done. Generally an affable sort, there are a few things that get her angry; and when angry, she is formidable. Probably not the world's best housekeeper, but she has many other good qualities.

You Are Like a Scent Hound

Keep a little pad in your pocket to jot down ideas that spring to mind or tasks you are given, otherwise they may not circle around again for a week. This group includes more than one "absentminded professor" able to get lost for days on the trail of a good idea. Example: Sarah once missed a plane while sitting at the gate. Reading a good book, she was lost in the pages, and when she looked up, everyone around her was gone, including the desk attendants. That is a Scent Hound and, by the way, her father is one, too.

Sight Hounds

Dancin' with myself

Your Significant Other Is Like a Sight Hound

For God's sake, don't leash him! Save the drama for your mama, 'cause this guy is likely to just walk (or run) away. A sensitive flower, he gives truth to Lincoln's point that you haven't converted someone just because you've silenced him. He loves to be comfortable, so give him a massage and get him soft/warm things if your climate is cool or cool comfort in the hot zones.

You Are Like a Sight Hound

Try to keep in mind that not everyone is as sensitive or as perceptive as you. They aren't being rude or mean or callous; they really don't feel everything you do. You may be thin and athletic . . . or not, but regardless of your size or build, you have a natural grace. You may feel more protected from the world if you wear layers or heavy sweaters. Anyway, you like to feel cozy. Find a partner who doesn't take your need for private time as rejection, and one who fights fair, since you will have little ability to tolerate anything else.

Terriers

You talkin' to me?

Your Significant Other Is Like a Terrier

Pick a fight with her every once in a while just to give her something to do, and then don't you dare give her an easy win (but do let her win)! It's worth doing because (1) she'll be so smugly happy and (2) the makeup sex will be terrific. She meets most new people with her tail straight up, so don't be surprised if it takes a while for her to make new friends. But when she does, she'll defend them to her last breath.

You Are Like a Terrier

Put your tail down! (Tail carriage = attitude. The higher the tail, the bigger the attitude, and in the case of a terrier, MAJOR attitude.) Not everyone you meet is a potential opponent, and not every person enjoys tussling. Take up a sport that lets you work out some aggression—from tennis to rugby, racquetball to karate—because you need an opponent. Our hope is that if you find one in sport, you will leave the rest of us in peace. When you retell moments of conflict—your war stories—you smile with enjoyment, relishing your verbal one-upsmanship. You like to win and never back down (what other people might call compromise). Find a partner who enjoys your fiery personality (someone who calls you his "little pistol") and loves that soft, sweet, and surprisingly sensitive side you save for your special loved ones.

Personal and Property Guards

Play to win

Your Significant Other Is Like a Personal/Property Guard Dog

If your partner is mentally stable (a key feature of a good example of these types), then make some popcorn and enjoy the show. Slick, quick, with more than one trick—your partner can both charm and disarm. Oh, and never—ever—betray a Guard type; they will never forgive or forget. Ever. Really, we mean, *ever*.

Deadly in competition—be it sports or business or both—there is no such thing as a "friendly" game of anything. And women, if you start to win, mean it, because love does not conquer all with this type—he'll always play for keeps. He likes to dress well, believes in first impressions, has more than one pair of sunglasses, and his smile can make some people slightly nervous.

You Are Like a Personal/Property Guard Dog

Chill. Samurai really don't have a lot of employment options, and they didn't get laid much—so drop down a gear or three. Your intensity is either a gift or an isolating curse, depending on how you channel it. If you want to live for business, then go flat-out—you're made for it—but be sure you don't find yourself at age 60 regretting what you skipped over way back when. People say you "have an agenda" in an accusatory way, which confuses you: Doesn't everyone have an agenda? You're loyal to a fault and loving to those you trust. You're an excellent companion to anyone who either is so laid back they balance you or so intense and smart they can match you play by play. Not many can.

Nordic Sled Dogs

Love the one you're with / Born to run

Your Significant Other Is Like a Sled Dog

Then keep up. This is not a person you should let out to "do his own thing" because that could end up being someone else. She wants you to come with her on her wild journeys through the world. If you want steady, staid, and stoic—move along. If you want impetuous, impossible, and impish, step right up! Sled dogs have a wide view of things and a deep, primal intelligence. If there ever *is* an end to the world, you want to be in the backseat of this girl's car, going where she's going.

You Are Like a Sled Dog

Have pity on all the house-dog types who never get off the porch. For them, a run is an outing, not a calling. They crave home, while you crave roam. You try to be honest to all those hearts you break on a regular basis—when you leave, they can't say you didn't warn them. If your company needs a visionary and already has a good herding dog or two in the ranks to help keep you in line, a good Nordic guarantees three things: a belly laugh, out-of-the-box problem solving, and intraoffice complications. It's a "hire one, get three" sort of deal.

Flock Guards

Who goes there?

Your Significant Other Is Like a Flock Guard Dog

Relax. He's got you covered. In fact, he's got the neighborhood covered. Don't expect random gifts. What you get is the big stuff: his heart on a platter—because, when he gives it, that's the only way it comes, whole and forever. Don't toy with one of these guys—they take the word "love" very seriously. This is a steady, quiet presence who is willing to throw himself in front of a bus for you without a first thought, never mind a second one. A steady, sturdy centurion.

You Are Like a Flock Guard Dog

Buy a book of jokes and try to figure out why they are funny. You seriously need to lighten up. Yes, ne'er-do-wells could storm the house, but, really, that is not likely to happen today. Why not read a romance novel and not another true-crime tale or murder mystery? Get out, take a class, join a club—you have a tendency toward agoraphobia, which you need to fight.

COME AWAY WITH ME, MY PET

When asked whom they would rather take to a desert island—their mate or their dog/cat—57 percent of women answered . . . well . . . Guys, stay! Dog, come!

Draft/Rescue Dogs

Lean on me

Your Significant Other Is Like a Draft/Rescue Dog

Call Merry Maids, put a six-pack in the cooler, and rest easy. Whatever crisis might occur, your guy is ready to deal. Not the most protective mate on the block, but that's okay. You're much more likely to need a guy who can help when you cut yourself badly than one who can drive the bad guys out of the house. He's a really good, good old boy. The best kind: easygoing, friendly, sensible, and steady. Don't expect him to use the hamper or put the seat down or wow the crowd at *Dancing with the Stars* with his tango steps, but get over it—those things are minor in the scheme of things.

You Are Like a Draft/Rescue Dog

We know it's not important to you, but make an effort in the housekeeping department. There's time between first quarter and second to pop those empties into the recycling bin and hang up your jacket. You're what others call "the salt of the earth." It wouldn't occur to you to cheat on your wife or lie to a buddy; it's just not in your nature. If you say you're going to be there, you're there—on time and with whatever you promised to bring. You're great "Dad" material. We doubt you're single, but if you are, enjoy it, because you won't be for long! And for your family's sake, cut out the pizza once in a while and exercise. No one's asking you to zip on any formfitting latex for a jog—bowling's fun, isn't it? You'll live longer, and all your loved ones want that.

Toys
The only thing better than luxury is more luxury

Your Significant Other Is Like a Toy Dog

Bring home gifts of little (or large) luxuries. Dote on her. Get an adorable pet name for her that you'd be embarrassed for your friends to hear. Compliment her on her glamour—compare her (*favorably*, you fool) to a model. She'll fight with a lot of noise and fire, and she isn't very rational in this state, so tread carefully there. Walking away and waiting for her to calm down can be easier than trying to engage.

You Are Like a Toy Dog

Take a deep breath—not everyone in the world is trying to step on you. The best defense really isn't always a strong offense. Take up meditation, tai chi, or yoga to help stay centered and focused. Find a partner who will treat you as the prize you are and appreciate your gifts of loyalty, intelligence, and devotion.

Herding Dogs

Keep it moving!

Your Significant Other Is Like a Herding Dog

Keep her busy, for heaven's sake! You don't ever want her bored brilliance to bear down on you. Here's a relational hint: Just because she comes to you mulling over a problem, do not— listen carefully here: do *not*—attempt to fix it. As well intentioned as you may be, she'll hear it as an insult to her abilities, and you'll get snarked for your trouble. Sympathy and support, that's all she wants. Also, when leaving for a trip, just keep your head down and your ears back—once she has everyone in the car and you're on the road, she'll stand down, but until then, you could get nipped for any "needless delay" (read here: asking a question, making a cup of morning coffee, taking "too long" in the bathroom).

You Are Like a Herding Dog

Please find a hobby. Maybe three, and don't turn that laserlike focus on your family. Many a lawyer lives in the herding group, able to argue her case from several angles, switching with ease when a new approach is needed, and so lightning fast you don't always see them coming. Find a partner who can stay even and give you clear direction when you get riled up. You may not think you need it, but you do. Calming down isn't easy for you, so pick someone who can help you do just that. You can go, go, go into nervous exhaustion if you're not careful and . . . you're not.

IF MEN REALLY WERE "DOGS" . . .

Women might like them better. Exactly how serious and deep is a woman's attachment to her dog? Though society often diminishes the importance of this attachment, science is beginning to shed light on the remarkable and significant phenomenon.

In 2002, Susan Phillips Cohen conducted a survey that measured intimacy, psychological kinship, and bond with pets, in an effort to tease out how men and women differ in their intimacy with pets.

Cohen, working at the huge Animal Medical Center in New York City, surveyed 201 clients randomly. Just about everyone in the study described their pet as "a member of the family." But what do they mean by that, exactly?

She found big differences between men and women.

Women felt—are you ready for this?—"significantly" more intimacy with the closest pet than with the closest person in their lives.

Cohen found that having a partner or a child did not affect the strength of attachment to a pet.

The results make resonant a quote from British novelist Elizabeth von Arnim, who wrote in her book *All the Dogs of My Life* in 1936: "I would like, to begin with, to say that though parents, husbands, children, lovers and friends are all very well, they are not dogs." She continued, saying of dogs, "Once they love, they love steadily, unchangingly, till their last breath. That is how I like to be loved."

A Walk in the Park

Dog parks are springing up in communities across North America in a surge so strong that the *New York Times*[1] has taken notice. Dog parks offer a gathering place for dog lovers, a club to which a dog owner has instant access, and, oh yeah, a place for the dogs to stretch their legs.

In their best incarnation, they offer safe, fenced areas for off-lead play with other friendly dogs. At their worst, every untrained, uncontrolled, obnoxious animal in a 12-mile radius converges on the point because they need "exercise" and "socialization." Most parks? Some combination of the two.

Consider this: Greeting and playing nicely with unknown dogs is an unnatural behavior in canids. They generally form family groups and "aggress" toward or avoid all outsiders. While many modern dogs enjoy the dog park a great deal, some dogs neither enjoy nor benefit from it. And if your dog is dog-to-dog reactive/aggressive, do us all a favor and skip the public dog park. A dog at Vicki's park lost an ear to a known aggressive dog that the owner insists on bringing week after week.

Such owners are either Wardens who select dogs for their aggression and then believe they can control that aggression; Free Spirits who think if their dog just played with other

---

1   "Living the Good Life, Off Leash," C. J. Hughes, *The New York Times*, March 4, 2007.

"nice" dogs he'd get over his "fear" and stop attacking them; Bystanders who live in a state of perennial surprise at the behavior everyone else in the park knows is coming; or Image Makers who fully enjoy their dogs' aggression and don't care about the consequences.

The Miss Marple mystery series and the potboiler *Peyton Place* proved the point that you can see a microcosm of the world's kindnesses, vices, eccentricities, and passions in small, "sleepy" towns. Well, as all owners know, that goes double for the dog park. There isn't anything under the sun you don't see on display there at some point. So here's a little guide to some of our favorite dog park characters.

Field Guide to Dog Park Regulars

The Novice

LATIN NAME: Novus know-nothingus

IDENTIFYING MARKINGS: New dog, new collar with shiny new tag attached, new lead, slightly confused and unsure expression, and sporting flip-flops, pumps, or some other inappropriate footwear

BEHAVIOR: Two variations of this common species. They usually travel alone or with a mate. May arrive with information guns blazing, ready to tell everyone else what to do, what they've learned from the many books they have read and sites they have surfed. Ready to change a park's culture. (Ha! Good luck.) Or, at the opposite end of things, absolutely clueless sponges, ready to listen to anyone, even the park's most notorious gasbags. Everyone else witnesses this (from afar) and says, "Oh, that poor thing doesn't know what a know-it-all end of Expert Ted is yet."

The Bully

LATIN NAME: Perpetrator perpetrator

IDENTIFYING MARKINGS: Muddy pants, torn coat from multiple "friendly" home assaults. Dog (usually male) strains on lead as he drags owner to the park, so heavy breathing can be heard from a distance, giving others time to flee. For this reason, travels alone or with one or two of the same species.

BEHAVIOR: Walks to center of park, releases dog (or, if in a smaller, pen-type run, releases dog just prior to opening gate). Dog does what he always does: stampedes toward some unsuspecting dog and slams into him. While this is happening, owner is attempting to get the plastic tab off the lid of his take-out coffee.

Dedicated Chuckers

LATIN NAME: Tossus some-morus

IDENTIFYING MARKINGS: Carries bag or knapsack of gear, dog leaping at pocket that holds *the* ball; owner often sports a claw mark or two.

BEHAVIOR: These owners of athletic, fetch-obsessed dogs come to the park ready to throw. They often claim a less-used area for their activities, making them one of the few territorial park types. May be equipped with a hard plastic ball "chucker," and if a swimming hole is available, may set up there. It's a Lab's wet dream.

The Mayor

LATIN NAME: Acceptus for-who-we-are-ium

IDENTIFYING MARKINGS: Well-dressed and well-mannered, without a paw print, stray dog hair, or a splash from a carried coffee, she (or he) somehow always manages to look fresh and put together even in the rain or at 6:15 a.m.

BEHAVIOR: Can be spotted easily circulating among park groups with a smile and a warm hello. (He actually knows the names of owners here—not just the dogs' names. Quite unusual in this setting.) His dog is as stable as the person, getting along well with every new group. One of the few types without an obvious allegiance or territory because the whole park is "his" and everyone in it a friend.

The Cop

LATIN NAME: Parkum bouncerius

IDENTIFYING MARKINGS: Has a big dog, but one that is well controlled. Regardless of size (or gender), oozes testosterone and a quiet authority. Denim, leather, cotton, and wool are his (or her) fashion fabrics.

BEHAVIOR: A good egg, and fearless, too. May hang around the edges or not take the lead in a group, but if—okay, when—a fight breaks out, the cop is there, wading in and keeping the peace. This is a good person to know and stick close to.

The Party Planner

LATIN NAME: Confero chardonnayus

IDENTIFYING MARKINGS: Big smile, and—a rarity at most parks—may sport a bit of makeup. Clean, matching ensembles, and maybe even a sporty, park-appropriate "messenger" bag over her shoulder. Avoid eye contact with this one, or you may be volunteered before you know it.

BEHAVIOR: Attempts to get park "working together" for a day of "good fun." Prints out sign-up sheets, carries several pens, and gets so involved trying to get you "on board" that she misses the fact that her Cavalier, Cocker Spaniel, or Golden Retriever is out rolling in something vile.

Who Me?

LATIN NAME: Pilus ignorus

IDENTIFYING MARKINGS: Wide variety of markings and decoration. The most obvious identifying feature? The absence of any plastic bags or newspaper for pickup.

BEHAVIOR: No matter where her dog defecates, she is always looking the other way, walking away, or turning her back to her dog. She ignores it so carefully that you know she sees what's happening. When offered a poop bag, she glowers and walks off. She doesn't "do" doo.

The Macchiato Mod Squad

LATIN NAME: Espressio elitus

IDENTIFYING MARKINGS: Cardboard coffee cups—lots of coffee cups.

BEHAVIOR: A territorial group, they stand in the center (physical or psychological) of the park, smelling strongly of hazelnut. Have complex greeting rituals that can be so engrossing that they completely forget their dogs . . . wait a second . . . what dogs? Where are their dogs?

Absentee Owner

LATIN NAME: Circumventio walkus

IDENTIFYING MARKINGS: Elusive inhabitant, no known markings. The only sign they have been around is the presence and then absence of their dog.

BEHAVIOR: Drops the dog off at the park entrance and goes . . . to work, on errands, whatever.

Rampaging Retractables

LATIN NAME: Tangleonius perpetua excrucio

IDENTIFYING MARKINGS: Retractable lead, always extended to the maximum length, the dog charging against the end, gagging.

BEHAVIOR: The ability to tangle themselves, their dog, your dog, you, your best friend, the small bush, the poop-bag dispenser, and anything else in a 10-yard radius within a 3.5-second period of time. . . . Well, you get the picture. But they never get the picture! They are as desperate to be with you as you are to get away from them when you hear that whizzing lead and speeding, manic dog charging up behind you.

Toying with Trouble

LATIN NAME: Minimus-doggeus riskus

IDENTIFYING MARKINGS: Frequently wears pink or white. Has a tiny, rhinestone lead attached to a tiny rhinestone collar attached to a tiny, anxious-looking dog. May carry a purse—an oddity in the dog park. Size does matter. Toy dogs in dog runs/parks go as well as toddlers on the field of an NFL game.

BEHAVIOR: High-pitched vocalizations accompanied by arm flapping when the Toy breed inevitably gets trounced by one or more larger dogs. Scolding tone if Toy breed attempts to defend herself.

The Jury

LATIN NAME: Matronae momentum

IDENTIFYING MARKINGS: Fashion à la Patagonia, Orvis, or L.L. Bean, maybe a little Eileen Fisher. Sensible and not inexpensive clothing with sensible and not inexpensive shoes. They live the phrase: There is no such thing as bad weather, just bad clothes. They know how to dress for walking success.

BEHAVIOR: These women power walk and power talk. They travel in pairs or small, rather well-dressed groups, and they don't miss a trick. They protect the underdogs and shun the bad guys.

Benchwarmers

LATIN NAME: Nonexertus geezeri

IDENTIFYING MARKINGS: Older owner (often overweight) with older dog (often more overweight) sitting on a bench in the sun getting some "exercise."

BEHAVIOR: Usually jolly, occasionally grumpy, members of this team probably know more about who's who in the park than anyone else. They just don't care to talk about it.

The Remodeler

LATIN NAME: Industria indomitus

IDENTIFYING MARKINGS: Fashion may vary. Look for the intense, earnest energy. When in his peak remodeling season, watch for attempts to make eye contact. Run!

BEHAVIOR: He always sees ways to improve the park: plantings, moving the bench, crushed stone at the entrance, mulch, and more mulch. Maybe an entrance fee to pay for a new path. Arggggh. More volunteer work for everyone. Petitions the Parks Commissioner . . . (You'd think he'd be friends with the Party Planner, but they despise each other!)

The Dog Walker

LATIN NAME: Funnius ruinius

IDENTIFYING MARKINGS: Easy, look for multiple dogs, poop bags sticking out of one pocket, leashes out of others, grubby sneakers, and jeans.

BEHAVIOR: Several subtypes of this species exist. One arrives at park, lets dogs loose en masse, and then can be heard running through the park yelling in a cell phone and at the dogs in turn—"Deb, I'll call you right back . . . Percy come, come, Percy come, no, Tabitha, no, wait, come . . ." A second subspecies frequents the smaller, urban dog runs. He enters, lets his charges go, and then leans back for a slow cup of coffee. Any chaos that ensues is ignored; any concern you have is ridiculous owner "overreaction." In general, you can confirm this sighting by the number of other owners who leave as soon as he arrives, not that he cares. He'd rather have the dog run to himself, anyway.

Excu-u-u-use Me

You've seen dogs behaving badly, and you've heard their owners providing some often "creative" explanations for all the jumping, humping, and bumping. You may even see similarities in people's excuses. Well, you're in good company. Social scientists have mapped it all out, finding that there is, indeed, a pattern of "excusing tactics" that dog owners employ. And—get this—it is nearly identical to that of parents dealing in public with misbehaving children.

The reason for the mirroring is that in both cases, a person is perceived as a "unit" with either the dog or the child. What the tyke or the Terrier does reflects on the parent/owner.

And when one misbehaves—according to a paper by Clinton R. Sanders, PhD—the social order is violated and the caretaker must take steps to reestablish his or her identity and standing. The paper, presented in *Anthrozoös*,[2] a scholarly publication on the human-animal bond, points out that the caretaker may feel "guilt, shame, or embarrassment," may see that his social standing is "degraded," and must take remedial steps to correct that.

The author was actually in the trenches—many of his observations were collected as he walked his own young Newfoundland pups. (What can we tell about him from his breed choice? For our money, he's probably a nice guy.) Sanders found that excusing tactics fell into seven categories (oh, how familiar they sound).

Situating

With this tactic, the owner blames the situation. You know, he's only acting this way *here*, nowhere else. "He gets scared at the vet," says the guy with the Chesapeake Bay Retriever in order to explain why the dog sounds like a revving Harley Davidson. "She's just excited," the Rottie mix's mom says as the dog hits a Golden pup broadside and bowls her over several times.

By making it situational, the owner is able to maintain a good opinion of the dog and reconcile this unwanted behavior with her mental image of her loved companion. This approach can be used to avoid addressing the issue since it is seen as limited and specific. Don't fall into that trap. Stress and/or excitement bring out things that may usually be hidden, but it rarely creates things from whole cloth. Use the opportunity for what it is—a chance to see the beginnings of a behavioral problem and do something to stop it.

2   "Excusing Tactics: Social Responses to the Public Misbehavior of Companion Animals," Clinton R. Sanders, *Anthrozoös*, vol. 4, no. 2.

Justifying

Blaming another dog or person—usually the victim. If one dog snaps at another, you might hear the owner say, "Your dog sniffed her too long," or "She doesn't like other dogs to get near dogs she likes," or as Vicki heard after a Labrador attacked her Wolfhound puppy—"Your dogs are just . . . too *big!*"

Again, the person is placing the behavior in a separate mental box, isolating it from her overall picture of her dog (who is smart, good, and loving, right?). Understanding the trigger of a behavior is fantastic! It shows insight and connection to your dog. But don't stop there—take action! Intervene, interrupt, redirect—don't let unfortunate things repeat themselves.

A common perpetrator in this category is the Buddy, who will lay out the classic comment (usually side-dressed with a slight "are you stupid?" intonation): "He's a dog." This is not an excuse and it certainly isn't an apology; it is a news bulletin for *you*. Buddies aren't especially prone to apology—and certainly not for what they consider to be patently obvious.

Behavioral Quasi-Theorizing

This is an attempt, according to Sanders, to "explain problematic situations and give them order and hope." And the contortions and lengths that people go to in order to do this are astounding. The explanations are rarely based on actual knowledge, but rather on convenient theories that get them off the hook. When a dog runs up to your picnic and goes facedown in the coleslaw, you may well hear, "He's a Beagle mix, he can't resist smells." Quite often, the owner who is being dragged down the street will say: "Oh, he's an alpha!" (This is often reported with a bit of pride—like, "My child has leadership potential!") This excuse doesn't make any behavioral sense, but it is nonetheless used universally for all manner of bad manners. "No," you might be tempted to call back, "he's no alpha; he's just untrained!" Who are the kings and queens of this particular excusing strategy? The Know-It-All Experts!

Processual Emphasis

Also related to quasi-theorizing, this tactic asserts that the behavior is temporary (in process). Either the dog in question is still just a puppy and will grow out of it (we hear this a lot when dogs jump up on people—and there seem to be a lot of two-year-old "puppies" at dog parks), or it is a behavior the owner is working to stop—"We have a trainer, but he says that this will take some time."

This is an optimistic tactic, as it assumes the issue will go away and is workable, and it is often true. Pups do go through sensitive periods where they overreact to things, and training can take some time. As with all excuses, it can linger too long and be misapplied, but used well it can accurately describe a transient situation.

Demonstrative Disciplining

In an effort to manage the situation, Sanders says, owners will come over to correct the dog. The fact is that this is the very best "excusing tactic" possible. This is a responsible owner stepping in and doing what she should. The dog jumps up, then the owner walks over and has the dog sit. The problem with many owners, Sanders says, is that they sometimes want to make a show of the training and they end up overcorrecting in front of you—yelling at the dog, or yanking him off his feet with the leash. That is generally displaced aggression on the human's part. They are embarrassed by their dog's behavior, and embarrassment makes them angry, so they are rough with the dog. Nascent Masters may make this error in judgment, and Wardens don't consider it a mistake at all, but you may also see it in Idealists and Dynamos for whom doing the right thing in the right way is expected and lack of either is horrifying. They can feel terrible afterward and confused by their own actions.

Unlinking

As annoying as the Justifying category can be, Unlinking is worse. In this tactic, the owner separates himself from the dog. He "unlinks" the unit, saying the relationship is in serious trouble: He has tried everything, and nothing works.

This is the hopeless phase of dog ownership—the "I know this is a problem, but I've done all I can do" end stage. Consider this the verbal equivalent of ears back and tail tucked—"Please don't yell at me, I can't help his behavior." For some people, there is no such thing as a behavioral deal breaker. But for others, barking, aggression, or house-breaking problems may, sadly, signal that the end of that relationship could be near. We see this most often in Soul Mates (especially Projectionists), Experts, and Observers.

Surprised to see Soul Mate here? Don't be. A Soul Mate loves passionately but doesn't necessarily sign up for persistent problems. She's looking for a best friend, not a reoffending parolee. A dog with aggression problems particularly may overwhelm a Soul Mate. Each of us has preferences.[4] Not everyone wants to date a recovering drug-addicted human or rehab the chronic submissively wetting dog—we can't all be Angels. These preferences point to the importance of sorting out as much of this as possible before bringing a dog home.

We've also seen an alternate form of Unlinking in which the dog owner has unlinked from people. They really don't care that the dog has growled at you, peed on you, or knocked you down. They say, with a semantic shrug, "I've tried everything . . ." which translates roughly

4   Caution: If you find yourself repeatedly re-homing or being less than thrilled, you might want to review your expectations—they may be unreasonable.

Everyone enjoys a walk in the park.

into: "I love my dog, I don't love you so . . . bite me." Look to our Angels, Avenging Angels, and Free Spirits for this angle.

Redefining

Most of us have seen this one often. All you do is recast bad behavior in a positive way. The dog isn't a bully, he's an "alpha." When he lunges at the pocket you keep your treats in, he's not rude—he's "smart."

Surprise

There is one excuse that we think Dr. Sanders has not covered, and it is so common you can find T-shirts emblazoned with the phrase: "He's never done that before!" Emphasis is on either the "*never*" or the "*that.*" Often this is truthful and said with sincere dismay. But it can also be a refrain for people who seem to be able to hit the inner delete button, essentially erasing from their memory any incident in which their dog has behaved badly. For example: Fluffy chases small dogs at the park. Fluffy's owner thinks Fluffy is a marshmallow who "would never hurt a fly." So every time Fluffy chases after a small dog, the owner is truly surprised. She pipes up with "She's never done that before" with such regularity that fellow park goers roll their eyes, muttering to each other: "Sure she did, just last Saturday!" Benign Neglectors, Free Spirits, and Angels are the most common perpetrators.

Common Dog Park Syndromes

Behavioral Amnesia

THE SYMPTOM: Memory of dog's bad behavior is quickly erased and replaced with happier ones in which the dog was provoked or had noble intentions: "Yes, he bit Barley, but you know, Barley had it coming . . ." or "He was protecting your dog. . . ."

THE CURE: Therapy. Lots and lots of therapy.

Marley-&-Me-Itis

THE SYMPTOM: The worse the behavior, the prouder the owner: He ate the *entire* Thanksgiving turkey just before everyone got there! Or—He shredded the couch in the ten minutes I was in the shower! A Roche-Bobois no less! We had just gotten it delivered the day before after waiting six months for it! And my boss was on his way over!

THE CURE: A crate. But what fun would that be?

Trainer's Tourettes

THE SYMPTOM: When those darn recall commands just repeat on you—"Come . . . Come! . . . COME! . . . #$%%^&&! COME Dammit!"

THE CURE: A leash and a plan.

Déjà You

THE SYMPTOM: Your dog attacks other dogs or runs off over and over again, yet it's always a surprise.

THE CURE: If you're not careful, the cure could be injury.

PERSONAL AMBASSADORS

How friendly is your dog? The answer could have profound effects on you. The reasons may, in fact, be fairly complex, but several studies have shown a Rover ripple effect.

One study by Podberscek and Serpell, published in 1997, linked owner personality traits and level of aggression in English Cocker Spaniels. Owners of the most combative dogs were themselves more tense, less stable emotionally, and "undisciplined." Another 1990 study found that the friendliness of dogs matched the friendliness of their owners.

Lots of factors would come into play here—including how others react to your dog when you're out walking. When Vicki had Tess, a shy, aloof Wolfhound, she interacted much less with other dog walkers in the park than when she had Lacey, "the pretty sister who got me invited to the best parties." Other questions arise, such as: When we choose a pup, are we attracted to the one who matches our own level of friendliness? Might something in our own personality influence our dog's friendliness or aggressiveness? Does the dog's personality affect ours?

There's so much more to be studied, but logic tells us that if people are skirting our aggressive dog, or racing over to greet our friendly dog, it would indeed affect the way we perceive ourselves and the world around us.[5]

5   All this from page 34 of *Anthrozoös*, "Personality Characteristics of Dog and Cat Persons," 1998.

Mutthausen by Proxy

THE SYMPTOM: The tiny bout of diarrhea is colon cancer. The puke spot on the rug signals the start of pancreatitis. A stumble at the park is neurological in nature. Your healthy dog, according to you, is always on the verge of medical disaster.

THE CURE: What? There's a cure? That must mean I was right; he really was sick!

Bully Blindness

THE SYMPTOM: Your dog humps everything in sight. Races up to people and other dogs and then knocks them over. Intimidates dogs, growls at them, is always in a fight. But according to you, "He just wants to have fun!" "He wants to play!"

THE CURE: Another, even meaner dog who picks on your dog. Suddenly that behavior doesn't seem so appealing.

New-Moania

THE SYMPTOM: The person is breathless to tell you the *best* vet, *best* food, *best* trainer, *best* daycare, *best* . . .

THE CURE: Meeting another YAPPIE (young, anal pet person)

Pandemonium Paralysis

THE SYMPTOM: Watches his dog obsess over, chase down, or harass other dogs, but does nothing.

THE CURE: Take your inner remote off "pause" and do something.

Conclusion

When we started *Dogology*, we both had our "favorite" types—the ones that matched our loved ones and us most closely. Then, through the journey of explanation, we were slowly wooed. We grew fond of them all—found a piece of many in our souls that we were not expecting would resonate. Those discoveries, often surprising, sometimes a little uncomfortable, were always delicious, as insight tends to be.

Before we leave you, we want to remind you of something. There are currently 44.8 million American homes that have a dog cohabitating within[1]: hogging the couch, tipping over the trash, getting muddy paw prints on the floor, and making our lives richer, more secure, happier, just plain better.

There are now more homes with dogs in them than with children (32.8 million households).[2] Love that fact, hate that fact, it's a fact. Given that, of course the way we attach to our animals means something! How ridiculous to think that it wouldn't or that strong attachment is a sign of some sort of "problem" in the person. When we number as we do, in the millions upon millions, we simply have to be seen for what we are: a mass of humanity—unique, varied, normal.

When such massive numbers of people participate in something, clearly there are real benefits to be had. We do not question the necessity of human friendship, or even how

1 http://www.appma.org/press_industrytrends.asp.
2 http://www.census.gov/prod/2001pubs/c2kbr01–8.pdf.

millions of people focus on sports (which we could argue is compensating for something). So how is it that attachment to animals receives such a persistently dismissive assessment in some circles?

We are not sure. What we do know is that when change does come to the way society sees a group, it is often rocky and the group doing the changing is not infrequently branded with some unfortunate label.

But do we care?

Not at all!

Consider this: Only 26 million to 37 million people in the United States play golf.[3] No one would claim that the gifted Tiger Woods and his laserlike focus on a tiny white ball is a sign of some underlying problem.

And we outnumber golfers by many millions!

So, revel in your doggy-ness, stand tall, be proud. Wag, even.

We picture *Dogology* giving voice and meaning to tens of millions. We see personal ads: Idealist looking for her Observer. We picture friends leaning across the table at Starbucks exchanging knowing glances: *It'll never work; she's such an Image Maker! His Buddy will never stand for it.* We want all you Macchiato Mod Squads across the country laughing communally and nodding when a Rampaging Retractable enters the park, or when a Bench Warmer settles down in the sun, sharing a Danish he doesn't really need, but always enjoys, with a dog who doesn't need it either, but always just says, "Yes, please!" without judgment.

Let's face it, in today's world of airbrushing, instant tanning, and the barrage of images of make-believe people living make-believe but richly affluent lives, no one gets out of our culture feeling great about themselves. Everyone sees where they miss the bar: Too heavy, too short, don't earn enough, not smart enough . . . whatever—everyone sees it but our dogs. To them, we are the perfect example of what it is to be human. We can find peace in their eyes, strength in their acceptance, joy in their greetings. It is their very doggyness that makes us better people.

---

3   http://answers.google.com/answers/threadview?id=415151.

And if mental health is just a toss of a tennis ball away, isn't that something to celebrate? Isn't that worth examining to discover exactly why dogs are so healing? How dogs can touch us as other humans simply cannot and probably never will be able to?

From *Dogology* we want you to gain pride in your attachment, to wonder at how it works, and to continue your deep enjoyment of this astonishing other species who has walked with us nearly since the beginning of time and will be with us to the very end. They would have it no other way. We would have it no other way.

About the Authors

Vicki Croke has spent more than 20 years covering animal issues in print and broadcast media, traveling to East Africa, the Galapagos Islands, the Arctic Circle, Tasmania, and Madagascar. She anchors a half-hour show on animals for NECN-TV in Boston. Her book *The Lady and the Panda* (Random House), which received critical acclaim, has been adapted for film by Michael Cunningham for Focus Features. Croke's other books include *The Modern Ark: Zoos Past, Present and Future* (Scribner) and *Animal ER* (Dutton).

"Animal Beat," her column on wildlife and pets, ran for 14 years in the *Boston Globe*. Croke has written for numerous publications including *Time, People, Discover,* the *Washington Post, International Wildlife, Gourmet, Prevention,* the *Sunday Telegraph of London, Popular Science,* and *O, the Oprah Magazine.*

As a contributor to NPR's environment show *Living on Earth,* she has reported on topics ranging from gorilla conservation to a coyote vasectomy. Her television work includes a 2-hour documentary on gorillas for A&E Television Networks.

Her entire career has been one big excuse to pat as many animals as possible.

Sarah Wilson has made it her mission, for the past 20 years, to teach people how to have fun while training their pets. She's done that in person, on TV and radio, in magazines and books, and over the Internet. Her TV work includes Comcast's *Pets On Demand* and Nick Jr's. *A Pup Grows Up.* Her popular training books, written with her husband, Brian Kilcommons, include *My Smart Puppy, Childproofing Your Dog,* and the now classic *Good Owners, Great Dogs.* They've been translated into German, Japanese, and Polish. With Brian, Sarah has also written more than a dozen articles for *Parade Magazine,* and her print list includes the *Boston Globe, Philadelphia Inquirer, Cosmopolitan, Trends, Pet Health, W, New York Newsday, Parenting, Dog World, Dog Fancy, Woman's Day, Dogs in Canada, Trends, The Healthy Dog,* and *Prevention.*

Sarah is on the advisory committee for the Animal Rescue League of Boston's Center for Shelter Animals. Pet owners and other professionals travel across the country to attend her seminars. Passionate about helping people live with and enjoy their animals, Sarah hopes her enthusiasm is contagious. She can be reached at MySmartPuppy@aol.com.

Photo Credits

Index

Boldface page references indicate photographs. <u>Underscored</u> references indicate boxed text.